Europa

Lutz Hübner: Born in 1964 in Heilbronn. He trained as an actor and was subsequently engaged at several German theaters. Since 1996 he has been a freelance writer and director in Berlin, where he lives with his family. He has written forty plays, which have been translated in twelve languages. Currently he is the most played living German playwright.

Tena Štivičić is a playwright, screenwriter and columnist. She holds a BA in Dramaturgy from the Academy of Drama Art in Zagreb and an MA in Writing for Performance from Goldsmiths College, University in London. Her award-winning plays have been produced across Europe and translated into a number of languages. Her play Seven Days in Zagreb was the Croatian partner in the ETC Orient Express international project in summer 2009. Her 2011 play Invisible, commissioned by Transport and the New Wolsey Theatre is currently in film development with Good Films.

Małgorzata Sikorska-Miszczuk is a playwright and screenplay author. She graduated from Warsaw University after studying Journalism, Political Studies and Gender Studies. She is also a graduate of Screenplay Studio at The Film and Theatre Academy in Łódź. Her plays have been translated into English, German, French, Serbian Croatian, Czech, Russian, Romanian, Ukrainian, Swedish, Spanish and Hebrew. Readings of her plays have been held in Poland, Germany, France, Sweden, Czech Republic, Russia, Romania, Belgium, Spain and the USA.

Steve Waters was born in Coventry in 1965 and studied at Oxford in the 1980s; his many plays include 'World Music' (2003), 'The Contingency Plan' (2009) and 'Little Platoons' (2011); he has written extensively for British theatre and radio. He currently teaches creative writing at the University of East Anglia and published 'The Secret Life of Plays' in 2010. He has written for 'The Guardian' and 'The New Statesman'.

Caroline Jester is a writer, dramaturg and educator and uses playwriting as a tool in many settings. She was Dramaturg and Literary Manager at the Birmingham Repertory Theatre for twelve years where she worked with many writers at all stages of their careers. She is a Fellow of the Institute of Creative and Critical Writing at Birmingham City University and a Master on the MA in Dramatic Writing at Drama Centre London. Caroline has also taught at Salford and Birmingham Universities, the Arvon Foundation and for the British Council. She is the co-author of 'Playwriting Across the Curriculum' (Routledge 2012) and the originator of REPwrite, an interactive playwriting zone. Caroline designs playwriting programmes nationally and internationally as well as developing her own writing, which includes translating 'The Wedding' by Bertolt Brecht for the Birmingham Repertory Theatre and site specific audio drama documentaries for the Museum of Carpe'

Małgorzata Sikorska-Miszczuk, Tena Štivičić,
Lutz Hübner and Steve Waters

Europa

Edited by Caroline Jester

*This edition contains the original script featuring dialogue
in the German, Croatian, Polish and English languages,
and the English translation of the script*

B L O O M S B U R Y
LONDON • NEW DELHI • NEW YORK • SYDNEY

Bloomsbury Methuen Drama
An imprint of Bloomsbury Publishing Plc

50 Bedford Square	1385 Broadway
London	New York
WC1B 3DP	NY 10018
UK	USA

www.bloomsbury.com

Bloomsbury is a registered trade mark of Bloomsbury Publishing Plc

First published 2013

British Library Cataloguing-in-Publication Data
A catalogue record for this book is available from the British Library.

ISBN: PB: 978-1-4725-2730-1
ePub: 978-1-4725-3021-9
ePDF: 978-1-4725-3149-0

Library of Congress Cataloging-in-Publication Data
A catalog record for this book is available from the Library of Congress.

Typeset by Mark Heslington Ltd, Scarborough, North Yorkshire

Europa

The world premiere of *Europa* took place at Zekaem (ZKM) in Zagreb, Croatia in April 2013, before touring to Dresden State Theatre in Germany; Teatr Polski Bydgoszcz in Poland and the Birmingham Repertory Theatre, UK. The project was funded with support from the European Commission.

Introduction

'Dear English, Scots, Welsh, Northern Irish and new British citizens, we want to continue having you on board,' said Germany's President Joachim Gauck at a speech in February 2013 on Europe's future. 'We need your experience as the oldest parliamentary democracy, we need your sober-mindedness and your courage.'

Kate Connolly reported in the Guardian (23rd February 2013) that the German President felt 'to encourage a greater sense of commonality, Europe needed a common language as well as encouraging multilingualism. "I am convinced that, in Europe, both can live side by side . . . The sense of being at home in your mother tongue, with all its poetry, as well as a workable English for all of life's situations and all age groups".'

One Language

It became apparent at the beginning of this journey that was to become the play 'Europa' that any exploration around European identity couldn't solely be examined from the perspective of one language. Language is intertwined with national identity and as the continent of the European Union is multilingual, how important is understanding our fellow European citizen in their own language? Do we all need to become polyglots in order to successfully coexist? Joachim Gauck seems to be using the dominance of the English language as a bargaining power here, to entice the United Kingdom's Prime Minister David Cameron into staying in the European Union when there is much current debate within the country as to whether it would be better for the nation if it left. Language is alive, a power within itself that can unite and fragment continents it appears. Germany's President in his speech seems to be saying that all groups within the European Union should know or learn some English to be able to deal with 'all of life's situations'. Are we all expected to learn English to become true European citizens? Many countries that are now part of the

European Union and older generations weren't taught English at school. Many also don't want to speak English in their own countries and why should we always assume we'll be fine if we travel anywhere within the European Union if we know this language? That wasn't the case on our travels for Four Cities, Four Stories, the name of the project that developed into 'Europa', and we only travelled to Dresden in Germany, Bydgoszcz in Poland, Birmingham in the United Kingdom and Zagreb in Croatia. And what about the many languages that are spoken within single nations? In a very short time Polish has become the second language within the United Kingdom since Poland's entry into the European Union in 2004 but going into inner city schools in the United Kingdom will reveal that there are many more languages being spoken within any one classroom. We can't ignore the question of language when discussing our European identity, and this project and production was an experiment to explore what would happen when four leading writers collaborated in four different languages that wouldn't normally find themselves all together in one room. Would a new language emerge that facilitated our understanding of our fellow European citizen, or would the barrier of strange words fragment and distance different cultures?

In 2009, whilst Dramaturg at Birmingham Repertory Theatre, I was aware of the growing debate around European identity within the United Kingdom as the political parties geared up towards the general election the following year. The European Union and the growing crisis of the Eurozone began to saturate the media and an increasing narrative around national identity within the fragmented nation that is the United Kingdom was taking central stage. The narrative has continued to develop over the last four years as most political parties are suggesting the need for a referendum after the next general election to decide whether the United Kingdom should stay in the European Union. How important is language to this debate around one country's national identity? One hundred and eighty nationalities live in Birmingham, England's second city so why is there little, if any cultural offerings in other languages that reflect and embrace its inhabitants? London is said to encompass more than two hundred and seventy nationalities and three hundred languages.

Many Voices

Theatre is a living artform and as such reinvents itself when faced with external pressures, which often become its driving force for retaining its place as one of the oldest surviving artforms. Multi-authored plays are a way of exploring new dramaturgies that have the potential to embrace our diversities whilst challenging the supremacy of the single authored piece. Collaborating is a way of confronting the questions we might sometimes avoid asking and help us to develop empathy. Theatre is a collaborative artform but playwriting is often a solitary process. A single authored approach didn't feel enough to embrace this subject matter so the idea to develop a multi-authored piece that could connect with 'European' audiences had to include more than one playwright and surely had to be in more than one language. The idea for *Europa* was born and the search for the writers who could embrace this challenge was on.

Lutz Hübner, Małgorzata Sikorska-Miszczuk, Tena Štivičić and Steve Waters are all leading playwrights in their respective countries, Germany, Poland, Croatia and the United Kingdom and met for the first time in Birmingham to discuss the idea. What became apparent from this first meeting was that there was a common experience between the writers from Germany, Poland and Croatia of exchanging practice through European co-productions, festivals and an awareness of a theatrical landscape that the United Kingdom wasn't really party to. Steve Waters in his blog for the Guardian wrote (13th December 2011):

'When I first met my playwriting counterparts last year I was struck by how narrow my horizons were and how extensive theirs was. While they seemed privy to a polyglot Euro-theatre in a number of nations, I was marooned in my own parochial setting, obsessed with a circuit of a few English theatres. And certainly the English theatre is hardly groaning with European plays.'

This became one of the driving forces behind this idea, a way of including the United Kingdom in this Euro-theatre through the creation of a writer-led piece that had an artistic cultural exchange at its heart. 'European' theatre has a reputation for being director led, so maybe a more writer led approach could be a way of enabling the United Kingdom's entry into this 'Eurotheatre', whilst 'encouraging a greater commonality' and multilingualism? Could the collaborative process be the common language that emerged? Leading producers Dresden State Theatre, Teatr Polski Bydgoszcz, Zekaem (ZKM) in Zagreb and the Birmingham Repertory Theatre bought into this idea and we began to plan its delivery and a successful application for funding from the European Commission for Culture followed.

The Wider Community
This journey had an unknown destination but connecting with as many people as possible through questioning was central to finding new avenues and routes into the material. The writers began by selecting ten questions that they wanted to ask citizens in their countries.

1 Name three rules Europeans live by

2 If you had to build a temple for Europe what would it be constructed from?

3 Congratulations! You get to host European 'Come Dine with Me'. What will your three course menu be?

4 The European Constitution is reduced to one sentence: what is it?

5 A Day for Europe – what, when and where?

6 When do you feel European?

7 How can Europe survive?

8 Who controls Europe? Who should control Europe?

9 Explain the European crisis to a child.

10 Congratulations! You have won a weekend break in Dresden, Bydgoszcz, Birmingham or Zagreb. Which one will you choose and why?

As well as the questionnaire being intended as a way to engage the general public with this project, the process was also the beginning of connecting the writers with the huge subject matter they were about to embark upon exploring. Deciding on the final questions generated much discussion but the process of questions began to create certain themes and a tone for the final piece that was already rearing its bullish head. A tone that was humorous but wasn't afraid to tackle areas that were sensitive and explosive. With hindsight, Europa was already present, observing this very process and beginning to explore what had become of her and whether she wanted to stay on this journey into an unknown future.

All four of the theatre companies involved have a strong connection with their local communities as well as having significant national and international reputations. Whilst this project had at its core the multilingual play that would be produced in all four countries, a community engagement programme was designed that not only enabled the writers to connect with diverse members of communities in each country but fed into the ideas within the script. This programme generated its own responses to the ongoing question about 'European identity' and began with visits to each city. The writers had up to this point used English as the working language, reinforcing the German President's remark, but as we entered each city it soon became apparent that we had to embrace all languages if we were to gain any insight into this 'European' world.

Dresden

The first stop on the map was Dresden on February 14th 2012. Unbeknown to everyone apart from the German partners, this is a significant day in Dresden's calendar. We were aware of the anniversary of the bombing of Dresden in the Second World War but we weren't aware that each year members of far right movements come to Dresden to remember the many killed in these bombings. They are met with much opposition and citizens join hands and turn their backs to try to stop them entering the city. Matthias Neutzner, a local historian was cited by George Packer in The New Yorker (1st February 2010) as saying:

'Dresden is a huge theatre stage, once a year, all different movements connected with European history and European identity use the stage to express themselves.'

In 2012 they were successful in stopping the unwanted visitors from entering Dresden, through their solidarity. This huge theatre stage that is Dresden was our starting point to see what connections with European history and European identity we could make for the play. Dresden State Theatre has an impressive connection with its citizens and actively connects members from diverse social groups through die Bürgerbühne, Citizens' Stage. Lutz Hübner and Beret Evensen, Dramaturg at Dresden State Theatre led a workshop with members of the Bürgerbühne aged 18 to 80. This cross generational workshop had diversity as its premise because of the huge disparity in life experience between its participants. The youngest members were born after the fall of the Berlin Wall and have always had freedom of movement across Europe but some of the older members literally found themselves in the centre of various partitions as countries were divided during the former separation of East and West Germany. Themes and words started to repeat themselves, borders, no borders, language, money, chaos but when asked if there was a European language a wonderful tale of a woman dancing her way across Europe with dancing partners in each country emerged. The other story of being at the centre of partitions had made a mark in Hübner's mind and would later find its way into the final script in the character of the German.

Bydgoszcz

Next stop Bydgoszcz and with the German woman's reminiscences of dancing still fresh in our minds we were treated to a Zumba demonstration by senior citizens at our first stop in a day centre for local elderly residents. Zumba is a recent craze to sweep the world and once again movement and dancing united our languages and connected the generations. Questions that then led to a discussion included:

'Do you remember a moment in your life when you were proud to be European – or were ashamed to be European'.

Stories emerged and the other cities started to be connected through personal experiences as some had family living in Birmingham and over lunch the Manager of the centre was keen to find her own ways of connecting the cities through community projects as she wanted to take her visitors to the centre of Dresden for a bonnet parade.

Łukasz Chotkowski, Dramaturg at Teatr Polski Bydgoszcz set up the next meeting with wives of people working at the NATO base in the city. This was to explore how foreigners felt in a city that doesn't have English for the majority as a European glue. How do you maintain your culture in a foreign city when there is the barrier of language? A Greek participant described how when she arrived in Bydgoszcz a Polish woman was talking to her and she said in English that she couldn't understand Polish but the woman continued in Polish. The woman tried again to explain that she couldn't understand but this time used her mother tongue Greek and the Polish woman then understood and this broke the ice. Not because she could speak Greek but because there was an authenticity in their communication through their own languages. They weren't bringing in a third party in the form of English to communicate. So English here wasn't able to help with 'all of life's situations'.

Another woman stated:

'Europe is an adolescent – not a child, not an adult and we have to define what it is.'

Workshops with cross generational actors raised similar themes around borders that had been present in Dresden but without losing the uniqueness of that city and country's experience and connection to the European Union. All could remember Poland joining the EU, some were children but all had the experience of a life before and after its membership. One of the younger members replied when asked if we needed someone with a vision for Europe:

'People are bored of the hero now, there's a new movement – everyone can be a leader. When there's no leader we must do something about it.'

Birmingham

A short direct flight from Bydgoszcz to Birmingham on a budget airline offered its own inspiration as Steve Waters began drafting scenes that would fight for their place in the final piece. In Birmingham the first group were primary school children, looking at when the word Europe begins to infiltrate our vocabulary. We discovered Poland was in Wales, Germany was near Belgium and Croatia was in China. Next stop the young professionals who felt Europe was over there, over the water. Our final destination in the heart of the United Kingdom was a discussion with a group of Asian Women who considered Birmingham to be a European city and that Europe is tolerant of different religious beliefs.

Zagreb

Final destination Zagreb, April 2012, one year before it became a member of the European Union. A workshop with actors and members of ZKM's youth theatre, which has over 1000 members. Cross generational, as in Germany and Poland, offering the insight into a country that has experienced its own continent in the form of the former Yugoslavia so would it offer any advice to the European Union and were its citizens happy to be joining another one? Language became central to this meeting with games being played in words in other languages showing how language evolves as other languages begin to infiltrate. Lots of German words are found in Croatian but it emerged that it was the syntax that made them Croatian, not the words. One participant felt excluded from some conferences she had attended with fellow European colleagues because her English wasn't as proficient and that when she travelled people don't know anything about Croatia.

'It's not surprising there's a problem with identity because history has been wiped out twice and that's when I realised me, my history was wiped out.'

This was too powerful to ignore. Croatians here felt European so there was a need to define what Europe is and what the EU is. Croatia's history is strongly asserted in the play through the character of Stribor and his attempt to get EU funding to tell the history of Croatia. More recent history is explored with subtlety in the scene in the shop selling Nazi memorabilia through the displacement and unity of the characters and language variances of Croatian and Serbian heritage.

Pulling Together
Whilst these experiences were a privilege to be part of the writers couldn't lose sight of the task at hand, how to turn all of this into one play in four languages. Would it become four individual plays held together by a common theme? A collage of scenes inspired by location and the characters that had been encountered along the way or would something emerge that went beyond exercises in collaborative playwriting?

But exercises in collaborative writing and sharing was an entry into exchanging ideas and work between four leading playwrights who had never worked together before. All have national reputations of excellence in their own right so how do you ask them to collaborate? There was the common experience of the journeys to all four cities and these permeated the writing workshops, often unconsciously. All writers began with five words each that they connected with Europe;

Jugendstil, Tram, Atrocity, Enlightenment, Landscape, Starts, Coffee machine, Regulations, Bank, custom control, Vla, Buildings with flags, Beach, Tips, Absturzangst, continent, Culture, Trees, War, Pleasure

Followed by word associations in each writers' own language to see what as an audience you can pick up in another language when you don't know any words. Each writer wrote a piece in their own language that started with,

What happened in Europe, when . . .

And the others had to say what had happened. Places, people and certain events were understood but what became apparent was that the tone of the story could push through, regardless of barriers to individual words.

Małgorzata Sikorska-Miszczuk took over the reins of the workshop and the energy shifted. Still unsure of each other's working pattern and writing process, she pulled out a set of cards. These weren't playing cards, but animal totem cards and invited each writer to select one and share these with the group. This wasn't the usual writing development process but as this was also a process of discovery and cultural exchange every writer took a card. Lutz Hübner picked the coyote, Tena Štivičić selected the elk, Steve Waters turned over to see a frog and Malgorzata revealed a bear. A map was being created placing these animals on their respective countries and a process of seeing which animal represented which part of the European Union followed. We returned to these animals when the scenes were delivered in the form of the Polish Shaman reminding the leaders of Europe to remember their ghosts. German Chancellor, Angela Merkel picks the coyote and wonders if Germany's problem is that it has become too serious and needs to embrace the trickster quality of the coyote. Croatia's Prime Minister Zoran Milanović selects an elk and begins to ask what has happened to the roar of the elk and why is its roar so quiet within the forest of Europe? David Cameron, Prime Minister of Great Britain chooses the frog and has to think whether he should start crying and ask for rain as tears cleanse the soul. When was the last time he cried? Finally the Prime Minister of Poland, Donald Tusk picks the bear and is invited to step onto the path of silence and calm his thoughts to listen for the answers.

The workshops had come to an end and the writers were left with the task of delivering three scenes in four months that were connected to or had the following within them:

Language, myths, cities, humour, trade, great leaders, a leitmotif, a song for Europe and ideas for games and pictures.

Four months later and over four hours of material was delivered. So how to choose which would survive into the next draft as the decision had already been made that the final production would be no longer than ninety minutes.

Europa and Zeus connected with everyone but at this stage it wasn't clear how and why. It opened up questions that helped to shape the final production, again with hindsight it's evident that Europa was playing an active role here. Some of the scenes worked well as one off scenes but some were returned to. A different cultural exchange between the writers was evident as some wanted to find the structure as a way of unearthing the narrative but others wanted to hold off making structural decisions as we would soon be joined by the director and actors. What did emerge again were key questions and statements that the writers responded to as a way of deepening their understanding of the text before sharing this with the rest of the creative team.

1 What's the magic word to open the door to Europe?

2 Europa's journey to the heart of Europe

3 Europa is looking for a home

4 Where have all the gods gone?

5 Where is Europe?

One response to the third statement was; 'She embodies this; the mother of Europe returns and no one recognises her'. Her presence was felt again as this became one of the central questions in the final piece but at this stage it wasn't recognised until new eyes looked at the text.

Drafting

A creative team was gathered that embraced the spirit of the project and was comprised of members from different countries. A Polish composer, Croatian designers, a lighting designer from the United Kingdom, two actors from each country and a director that could be classed as 'polyglot eurotheatre' himself, Janusz Kica. Janusz Kica is a Polish director who moved to Germany in the 1980s, works all across the continent and speaks all four languages fluently. This added a completely new dimension to the dynamic and exploration of language as for the first time someone who understood the nuances within each language equally was present, not someone who understood one or two languages and maybe a few words in another. How would the play stand up to this scrutiny and how would he approach this? Up until this point writers led the process but we were entering into the territory of the director led 'European' theatre. Would he communicate in each language to the individual actors? A weeklong workshop in Bydgoszcz followed, which involved much discussion as each artist observed and exchanged cultural practise as well as embracing this challenge of working with a multilingual text. Whilst the actors from

Poland, Germany and Croatia were more used to travelling and performing in different countries, this was a new experience for all actors as nobody had worked on a multilingual piece in these four languages before. The question of European identity was being explored through the very process of this artistic exchange. What emerged in this workshop was that the scenes written by Steve Waters could be used as a starting point to begin to cut the material. Could the scenes where artists are trying to sell their ideas for funding from the European Commission be the glue to hold the piece or would this be too much like art reflecting life?

I made the initial cuts and halved the material. All writers lost work and whilst there were no initial objections a deeper collaboration between writers began as the second drafts were due. Steve Waters and Tena Štivičić decided to write a scene together as in the initial draft there was an individual scene of a Croatian trying to sell the idea of the history of Europe. Stribor didn't want to leave the play and pushed his way into the scene with Astrid, Sunčana and Christopher and strengthened his voice and pushed the question of multilingualism further. Maybe Europa had something to do with this.

A weekend workshop was planned in Dresden to explore the second draft. Time was running out, decisions were difficult to make so two drafts were tried out. Lutz Hübner and Beret Evensen delivered a collage like version of the text to begin to structure this into a rehearsal draft and I brought another version. The German draft was the strongest in the rehearsal room and this led to key decisions being made. What did become clear at this stage was that the voice of the Shaman was getting stronger and his message was getting louder.

In the Rehearsal Room
Rehearsals in Zagreb began with Janusz taking charge and ready to bring his vision to the piece as he magically brought this play to life. 'Four Cities, Four Stories', became 'Europa' in his hands as he witnessed her presence and brought her

to prominence as she wasn't going to leave the stage throughout all of the performance. Her narrative was loud and clear as a world that was full of diverse characters fought their way to be heard in this 'Europe'. The Estonian 'pyro' artist circles the stage when she's not allowed to burn euros within the same play that we find Croatian Ana who is Muslim telling her story of falling in love and marrying her British husband of Pakistani heritage. This is interpreted at the same time by the authorities and she tries to speak louder to tell her side of the tale until she's visibly bound in tape as they are stopped at the border of the United Kingdom after a trip to Pakistan under suspicion of terrorism.

Scenes were fighting for survival throughout the rehearsal process and discussions led to national topics that emulated the play. Was there too much of one language in the play? Should the piece be cut with this in mind or was this compromising the artistic choices? Shouldn't there be more of languages that aren't heard that much within Europe? Why shouldn't the English actors speak in other languages?

Production
Kica's production was an exhilarating race through Europe and visually stimulating through its very contradiction. The stage was a bare room that became populated by disparity and an urgency to paper the walls with a European identity. Europa circled and watched, ever present to see how the continent is behaving and only exchanged glances with the Shaman who recognised her. In this production, Europa broke out of these walls but in another production she might choose to stay. What her presence does do in the play is remind us that if we don't behave respectfully we might not like the look of our offspring. She leaves us with this question and whilst she doesn't provide direct answers she reminds us of our need to keep questioning and communicating with our fellow citizens even if we don't always understand what they say initially.

This collaboration took the play further in its examination of this subject matter because of its multilingualism than it would have if it had used a 'workable English for all of life's situations and all ages'. The embracing of the unknown through this process was heightened because of the strangeness of words but it was the diversity yet commonality of spirit that was its success.

Europa

Characters in order of appearance

The original production had eight actors, two from each country, but the text remains flexible and can be interpreted in any way.

Offizier
Beamter
Europa
Sunčana
Astrid
Christopher
Szaman
Katya
Službeno lice
Ana
Stribor
Kobieta
Inozemno službeno lice
Ein Deutscher
Svetozar
Mušterija
Željka
English Actor
Aircraft Official
Putnik 1
Putnik 2
Putnik 3
Putnik 4
Putnik 5
Putnik 6
Putnica 7
Stjuardesa
Novinar
Novinar 2
Novinar 3
J2b1
Singers
English 1
German 1
German 2
Polish 1
English 2
Croatian 1
Polish 2
Croatian 2

Scene One

Offizier   OK, was haben wir. Unbegleitete Minderjährige mit Nutzvieh heute 7:48 von Patrouillenboot A 1653 vor der Westküste Kretas aufgegriffen, keine Papiere.

Beamter   Der Dienstleiter sagt, sie wäre auf einem Stier übers Meer geritten.

Offizier   Sehr witzig! Egal, hat sie schon Angaben zur Person gemacht?

Beamter   Nein.

Offizier   Wo ist der Stier?

Beamter   Unten im Hof, das ist ein ziemlich eigenartiges Tier.

Offizier   Also fangen wir an. Dein Name? Name? OK. Ich (*deutet auf sich*) Diebold (*deutet auf den Beamten*) Sikorski (*deutet auf Europa. Europa deutet auf sich.*)

Europa   Europa.

Offizier   Ja, schon klar, da wollen alle hin. Aber Name.

Europa   Europa.

Offizier   Hol doch mal den Dolmetscher.

Beamter   Welchen? Wir wissen ja nicht, wo sie herkommt.

Offizier   Land? Nation? Ursprung?

Beamter   Das kommt davon, dass die Araber ihre Mädchen nicht in die Schule schicken.

Scene Two

Der Offizier mit der Weltkarte, Europa versteht nicht. Er zeigt auf der Karte Europa.

Offizier   Europa.

Der Offizier deutet auf verschiedene Länder, deutet dann auf Europa.

Offizier Du?

Europa Phönizien.

Offizier (*zum Beamten*) Sie haben doch Abitur, wo ist das denn?

Beamter Ich google das mal.

Offizier Und der Stier? Ist das dein Stier?

Europa Zeus.

Offizier Da sind wir doch schon mal einen Schritt weiter.

Beamter Phönizien lag auf dem Gebiet des heutigen Libanon. Aber das ist dreitausend Jahre her.

Offizier Dann ist das mit der Minderjährigen schon mal Quatsch.

Scene Three

Sunčana *and* **Astrid**.

Astrid Oh, are you OK with German?

Sunčana Mein Deutsch ist nicht so gut. Englisch besser.

Astrid So English it is. So – you found us anyway. Your contact was Christopher?

Sunčana That's right.

Astrid And I think you're from Zagreb?

Sunčana Yes.

Astrid Hübsche Stadt. I lost my virginity in Zagreb.

Sunčana Well. Congratulations!

Astrid I have no idea why I just said that.

Astrid *laughs*.

But now you're in Brussels? Studying?

Sunčana I gave up my studies. Money ran out.

Astrid   Well . . . schade.

Sunčana   Yes. I live on ten Euros a day. It is possible.

She smiles.

Astrid   So I'm Astrid, Astrid Krause – I oversee Digital and Multi-media funding Europe-wide. Christopher oversees Intercultural Dialogue.

She laughs.

Sunčana   Why, why did you laugh?

Astrid   You'll understand when you meet him.

Sunčana   And today – the money comes from – for today?

Astrid   We have a budget under-spend. I think for the last time, actually. We need to spend it or lose it; if we lose it, people ask what we are for and then we lose our jobs.

Sunčana   So you spend it on art to keep your jobs?

Astrid   Yes – no – a slightly crude account!

She checks her watch.

Where is he? OK, we will start without him.

Would you mind taking notes?

Sunčana   My pleasure.

Christopher *enters eating a waffle; he waves at everyone, takes off his coat, arranges his notes.*

Christopher   Tut mir leid.

Astrid   You're late.

Christopher   Had to go to a funeral, all right?

Astrid   Oh. Well. I'm sorry, of course.

Christopher   They happen a lot when you're my age. Matter of fact it was lovely; in Shropshire.

Sunčana   Shropshire?

Pause.

Should I not ask questions?

Christopher   Is this something I should know about?

Astrid   It's the intern you emailed me about.

Christopher   Intern? I sent no such email.

Sunčana   I sent you my CV. Sunčana, hi.

Christopher   Right. You're sure of that?

Sunčana   Every day since I have emailed you.

Christopher   Yes, yes of course. The . . . Slovenian?

Sunčana   Croatian.

Christopher   My mistake.

Astrid   As we've had secretarial support cut it's fortunate she's here.

Christopher   Ausgezeichnet. Unpaid labour. Definitely the future of Europe.

Astrid   So maybe we can get going?

Christopher   Great to finally meet you Sun . . . cana.

Sunčana   Sunčana.

Christopher   'Sunčana' – yes, I was in Shropshire, yes, for a funeral.

Sunčana   Who died?

Christopher   Oh. My mother, actually.

Sunčana   I'm sorry.

Christopher   Don't be. It was . . . a kindness.

Yes, a beautiful event – she was a Humanist, these things can be quite embarrassing but I read some Goethe, we sang that aria from 'Cosi' – you know – 'Soave sia il vento'. Corny perhaps, but . . . very moving.

Scene Four

Szaman   Największym nieszczęściem Europy jest to, że przestała wierzyć w duchy. Europa wyśmiała swoje duchy i zapomniała o nich. Europa ogłuchła. Nie słyszy duchów. Duchy wody i powietrza, duchy Ziemi, duchy krokusów, byków i chimer przestały być słyszane i rozumiane.

Europa może również nie słuchać mnie. To mnie nie zniechęca. Jest moim obowiązkiem przypomnieć Europie o duchach.

Chciałbym, aby Europa, poprzez swoich przywódców, spotykała się w wielkim kręgu, gdzie nie ma ważniejszych i mniej ważnych. Chciałbym, aby krąg przywódców Europy zadawał pytania o przyszłość każdego kraju i Europy nie doradcom politycznym, ministrom finansów, Parlamentowi Europejskiemu i innym tego rodzaju osobom i instytucjom, tylko zadawał pytania duchom.

Scene Five

Astrid   If you don't feel up to this –

Christopher   What could be more of a tonic than meeting a bunch of artists?

Astrid   Sunčana, would you mind fetching in the first applicant? Thank you.

Sunčana *brings in* **Katya** *comes before them.*

Astrid   Katya. Live artist.

Sunčana   From Kuressaare, Estonia.

Katya   Yes. Hello!

Kuressaare. Yes.

Astrid   Hello Katya.

Danke für Ihr Kommen. Wenn Sie vielleicht kurz Ihr Projekt beschreiben könnten? Das wäre großartig.

Katya   OK. In Englisch?

Christopher *laughs.*

Astrid   English is fine.

Katya   Title: 'Fire Sale'. You receive details?

Astrid   We'd like to hear a bit more from you, the artist – and I should say, we are seeing a lot of people today so brief is great.

Katya   OK. OK.

Katya *pulls a lighter out of her pocket.*

Christopher   What's she doing?

Astrid   Keine Ahnung.

Now she pulls out a ten Euro note.

Katya   OK. Ten Euro note. So.

Astrid   OK, yes, we got that.

Now she ignites the lighter and sets the note alight.

Christopher   Actually, we have a smoke alarm in here. A very sensitive smoke alarm, notoriously hard to disable.

The smoke alarm goes off.

Astrid   You really need to stop burning things.

Sunčana   Are these real euros?

Katya   I make . . . 'pyre' – 'pyre'?

Christopher   Absurdly over-reactive.

Astrid   The criteria for the awards, the grants are largely based on 'Intercultural Dialogue', or, err, 'Embodiment of European Spirit' –

Katya   Excuse me, this is, this is better: 'FIRE-SALE – title – Europe: common denominator: MONEY'! Burn – dying currency, in burning, allow to be re-born? OK?

Astrid   OK, thank you, Katya.

We need to stop it there. I think.

Katya   Is all?

Astrid   We have your portfolio.

Katya   I come a long way.

Christopher   We cover expenses I think.

Katya   OK. OK. Bye, bye.

Hope you like 'Fire Sale'.

Scene Six

Szaman   Powtarzam: chciałbym, aby Europa, poprzez swoich przywódców, spotykała się w wielkim kręgu, gdzie nie ma ważniejszych i mniej ważnych. Chciałbym, aby krąg przywódców Europy zadawał pytania o przyszłość każdego kraju i Europy nie doradcom politycznym, ministrom finansów, Parlamentowi Europejskiemu i innym tego rodzaju osobom i instytucjom, tylko zadawał pytania duchom.

Każdy, na przykład kanclerz Niemiec, Angela Merkel, miałby możliwość zapytania duchów zwierząt o to, co jest potrzebne jej lub jego krajowi.

I oto Angela Merkel, w skupieniu i powadze, podnosi lewą dłoń i delikatnie przesuwa ją nad Kartami Uzdrawiającej Mocy z 52 zwierzętami, z których jedno odpowie na pytanie o rolę Niemiec w wspólnej Europie.

Angela Merkel wyciąga kojota. Patrzy na niego długo, a potem dziękuje mu.

Angela Merkel wraca do kręgu z wizerunkiem kojota w sercu. Od tego momentu wiele aspektów mocy kojota będzie dyskutowane w mediach całego kraju. Co oznacza wyciągnięcie tej karty? Autorytety moralne, filozofowie, naukowcy zaczną zastanawiać się wspólnie jaką naukę kojot oferuje Niemcom. Kojot to wieczny figlarz, szaleniec i trickster. Może to, co dolega Niemcom, to zbyt wiele powagi?

Jest tyle rzeczy, z których się można śmiać, ale nikt się nie śmieje, wszyscy są poważni. Dlaczego Niemcy przestały się śmiać? Dlaczego przestały się wygłupiać? Dlaczego tak trudno inaczej niż poważnie spojrzeć na sytuację? Co Niemcy niosą ciężkiego na sobie? Takie pytania zadaje sobie Angela Merkel. Myśli też o tym, kiedy przestała się śmiać z siebie samej. To wszystko jest zbyt poważne. Gdzie jest miejsce na żart i śmiech? Dlaczego nie mogłabym spłatać jakiegoś figla? Dlaczego nie mogłabym powiedzieć Hollandowi z poważną miną, że w wolnych chwilach tańczę na rurze? Albo że nocą domalowuję wąsy paniom na billboardach proszków do prania?

To są prywatne myśli Angeli Merkel, ale myśli ona też o całym kraju. Jak to się stało, że zrobiło się tak poważnie, tak grobowo poważnie. Czy Niemcy muszą być zawsze takie poważne? Czy zawsze musimy być odpowiedzialni? Nikt nie myśli, że możemy być błyskotliwi, zwariowani, szaleni. Dlaczego staliśmy się więźniami tak poważnego wizerunku? Może to nie jest smutny wizerunek, ale sztywny. Nudny. Dlaczego staliśmy się największymi nudziarzami Europy? Bogatymi nudziarzami. Po co nam to? Czy jesteśmy z tym szczęśliwsi? Czemu wszyscy oczekują, że Niemcy będą tacy odpowiedzialni? Czy to przyjemne być tym, który jest zawsze odpowiedzialny? Jeśli jesteśmy tym, który jest zawsze odpowiedzialny, to kto inny będzie tym, który jest zawsze nieodpowiedzialny.

Wtedy nie ma ma żadnej równowagi. To nie jest dobre.

Angela Merkel patrzy na przywódców innych krajów i widzi w ich oczach, że jeśli nie przestanie być taka odpowiedzialna, to inni będą zawsze nieodpowiedzialni. I widzi, że oni zaczynają rozumieć, że skoro Niemcy wyciągnęły kojota, to coś wymaga zmiany. I ta zmiana nadejdzie. Teraz Niemcy wezmą pałeczkę żartu, śmiechu i zabawy. Bo tak dalej być nie może. Bo Niemcom jest za ciężko. To nie jest przyjemne. To nie jest w porządku. To nie jest fair wobec Niemców.

Scene Seven

Službeno lice   Ana Esma Khan rođena je u Zagrebu 1979. od oca Munira i majke Marijane. Otac i majka upoznali su se na fakultetu političkih znanosti sredinom sedamdesetih godina. Otac Munir Omerpašić, za prijatelje Mujo, rodom iz Gornjeg Vakufa stigao je u Zagreb 1975. godine i na drugoj godini studija upoznao Marijanu Tot-Hladiku te je veza uskoro okrunjena brakom 1977. kad je Marijana bila u trećem mjesecu trudnoće s Aninim starijim bratom Tarikom. Ana Esma Omerpašić, rođena dvije godine kasnije, na majčino inzistiranje dobila je ime po baki Ani Tot. Brat Tarik naslijedio je pradjedovo slavno ime. U obitelji Omerpašić pronosi se legenda kako njihovo podrijetlo seže sve do Mehmed-bega Stočanina, utemeljitelja Gornjeg Vakufa, no malo je materijalnih dokaza koji bi poduprli tu tvrdnju, što je često bivalo predmetom razmirica između supružnika.

Ana   Mama je uvijek smatrala da je tata malo seljo. Kao i svi njegovi, pa taman bili i najplementije bosansko plemstvo. Ipak, kad bi bilo tko drugi zaustio da kaže koju na temu tatinog 'bosančeroskog' porijekla, mama bi se kao lavica bacala da ga obrani. A to je obično bila moja baka koja je i sama tvrdila da ima neko daleko plemenito ugarsko podrijetlo za što su isto postojali sasvim arbitrarni dokazi.

Nama je, bratu i meni, mama uvijek pričala što su sve muslimani doprinijeli našoj civilizaciji i o bogatoj muslimanskoj kulturi o kojoj nismo ništa učili u školi.

Ni mama ni tata nisu se molili ni bogu ni alahu.

Samo ponekad došlo bi do sukoba na religioznoj osnovi kad bi baka za nedjeljnim ručkom tvrdila da smo mi, Hrvati, uvijek bili predziđe kršćanstva, da nas je naš vjekovni prijatelj Papa još u 15.stoljeću nazvao Antemurale Christianitatem i da nije bilo nas, 'Turci bi nas pregazili, i danas bi se cijela Evropa pet puta dnevno klanjala istoku'.

Onda bi tata rekao da je baka pokondirena tikva i da se ne kaže Antemurale Christianitatem, nego Christianitatis, jer je to genitiv.

Ali, uglavnom, moj tata Munir, moja mama Marijana, moj brat Tarik i ja, Ana, mi smo svi bili Jugoslaveni.

Inozemno službeno lice   Mishal Khan was born in 1976, in Birmigham. His grandfather Malik Khan fought for the British Indian Army during the British Raj but it wasn't until 1954 that Mishal's father Hassan and his wife Saaida moved to the West Midlands. Mishal's father was a doctor and his mother a housewife. After settling in Great Britain they raised four children. Mishal, Fatima, Ahmed and Sanjiv.

Ana   Mojoj mami nije bilo drago kad sam srela Mišu. Veli ona 'Jebala vas ta muslimanska žica, pa ti si Zagrepčanka, kak si uspjela od cijelog svijeta nabasat na ovoga, nije mi jasno. I to ne jednog od ovih nasih musla. Ne. Baš pravog pravcatog. Vidi ga, srećom nemate sunca u toj Engleskoj, znaš kako bi se začađavio da ga je malo osunčat.'

Mama se cijeli život bojala da ću se zaljubiti u nekog iz onih zemalja gdje žene nemaju pravo glasa i da će me otfurati k svojima kao onu ženu iz 'Ne dam svoje dijete'. Pa kad sam upoznala Mišu mami se zamračilo pred očima. A bome i tata je bio malo skeptičan. 'Ipak smo mi Evropljani, mišu, znaš, a oni su ipak nešto drugo'. Kaže moj tata Munir.

Doduše, kad su se upoznali, moja mama je odmah pala. I ona i Mišo dobro govore njemački i vole literaturu, posebno indijsku. Pa onda satima bistre Rushdija i Kureishija na njemačkom i to mami daje osjećaj posebne važnosti. Jer moj tata, Munir, osim povijesnih knjiga, voli samo Andrića i Jergovića. Volio je i Aralicu, ali toj je ljubavi prošao vijek.

A moj Mišo, on bi čitao cijele dane. Vuče ga stalno nešto da shvati sebe i svoje i koji su to uopće njegovi. Mene je već dosta zbunilo ovo da sam prvo bila Jugoslavenka, a onda Hrvatica. Ali biti Pakistanac u Britaniji . . . još u ovo vrijeme . . . i osjećati tako duboku pripadnost jednom i drugom identitetu, ja mislim da je Mišo heroj. Mislim da mi se zato tako i dopao. Čovjek u kojem je uvijek neki pokret.

Scene Eight

Europa   Europa, Tochter des Königs, der seinem Land den Namen gab, Phönizien, Wiege des Geldes, Heimstatt der Händler, deren Schiffe segelten bis zu den Säulen des Herakles, Waren zu tauschen, in Gold aufgewogen in den Palästen ihrer Kindheit, eine goldene Jugend, Schönste der Schönen stolz und eigensinnig, die Einzige, die Widerworte geben darf Phoenix, dem liebenden Vater, Stern seiner Augen, Wachs in ihren Händen, Europa, die von Männern nur kennt den gebeugten Rücken im Thronsaal des Mächtigen und die schmeichelnden Stimmen der Eunuchen, ihr Leben am seidenen Faden ihrer Wünsche, ausgeliefert der Prinzessin heftigen Launen.

Scene Nine

Szaman   Premier Chorwacji, Zoran Milanovic, wyciąga kartę z łosiem i przechodzi go dreszcz. Łoś jest kwintesencją poczucia własnej godności. To jego moc, moc łosia. Co się stało z rykiem łosia? Czemu nie słychać go w europejskim lesie? Czemu milczy? Gdzie jego głos? Gdzie głos dumnego króla lasu, który dokonał wiele i obwieszcza o tym swym rykiem? – myśli premier Chorwacji. Gdzie jest nasza godność? Gdzie duma z naszego narodu? Co się z nią stało? Mądrość łosia jest mądrością doświadczonego wojownika, który długo wędrował, walczył, wiele widział i dokonał, i jest już członkiem starszyzny. Teraz czerpie radość z uczenia, dzieli się swoją mądrością. Może przestałem się uważać za mądrego? – myśli chorwacki premier. Może wszyscy Chorwaci przestali się uważać za mądrych, może uważają, że inne nacje wiedzą więcej od nich? Łoś wie, kiedy ryknąć. Czy tak się dzieje? – myśli premier Chorwacji. Czy wiemy, kiedy dumnie ryknąć? Czy jesteśmy otoczenie szacunkiem? Czy zadają nam pytania podczas narad?

Przecież nasza mądrość jest wielka, większa niż wydaje się innym członkom tego kręgu. Oni teraz patrzą na kartę łosia, którą wyciągnęła Chorwacja, i myślą, co to oznacza dla nich. Może tylko sobie przypisywali przywilej bycia mądrym? A ceremonia kręgu pokazuje, że jest inaczej. Może wszyscy powinni się zastanowić?

Scene Ten

Culture programme – **Stribor** *is setting up a presentation – the title in Croatian and English – The Stone is Burning the Wave is Frothing* (**Kamen gori val se pjeni**).

Astrid   Sunčana, can this fellow speak English?

Sunčana   Stribor has prepared the whole presentation for you in English in this folder.

Christopher   Do we even fund Croatian art yet? I mean are they on-stream?

Astrid   If it makes a positive contribution to European culture which I am sure –

Stribor   Šta kaže – we are not a positive contribution?

Sunčana   Samo se vi koncentrirajte na prezentaciju. Samo jasno i koncizno.

Christopher   Looks fiendishly complex.

Stribor   Yes. I am aware. But that's exactly what I think is necessary. Dakle, mulitmedijalni projekt Kamen gori, val se pjeni bit će dosad najopsežniji performativni projekt o povijesti hrvatskog naroda. Mi u produkcijskoj kuci Tuga i Buga smatramo da je vrijeme apsolutno sazrijelo za takav jedan projekt.

Sunčana   'The Stone is Burning the Wave is Frothing . . .' intended to be the biggest project telling history of Croatian people, never been tried before . . .

Stribor   Tema ovog projekta jest i razlog zašto ga dosad nije bilo – tj. nepouzdanost izvora kroz povijest pod tuđinskom vlasti koji dovode do nemogućnosti shvaćanja vlastitog identiteta.

Sunčana   . . . he even says the theme of this project is in fact why it is being done . . . err – unreliability . . .

Stribor   . . . Uneraliability, yes . . .

Sunčana   . . . of historical record which was in the hands of occupying powers making it impossible for us to understand our own identity.

Stribor   Maybe it is not good for Europe to bring into its . . . so to speak . . . organism . . . an . . . organ which it does not know. Ono što je posebni specifikum Hrvata kao takvih jest da su oni jedan od malobrojnih naroda, moglo bi se čak reći među jedinim narodima u Europi koji nikad nisu vodili osvajačke ratove.

Sunčana   What is particularly specific about Croats as such is that they are among the rare nations in Europe, maybe the only one, who have never waged wars of aggression.

Astrid   Ach, das wusste ich nicht. Interessant.

Sunčana   Stribor has apparently prepared a video presentation as a kind of a guide through the chapters of history.

A film starts to run with images of beaches on the Croatian coast and women in swimming costumes. Here is even Ana Sasso, emerging out of the water. There are also images of suntanned young men in swimming trunks.

Stribor   I am sorry. This is another presentation.

Stribor *fiddles with the laptop.*

Prvo poglavlje – 7. Stoljeće nove ere iliti poslije Krista – ovjekovječeno na ovoj poznatoj slici Otona Ivekovića –

Sunčana   Beginning of project shows arrival of Croats in country as shown in famous painting by Oton Ivekovic.

Stribor   Dolazak Hrvata na Jadran.

The painting appears on the screen.

Astrid   Can he tell us anything about his target audience?

Stribor   No, sorry, I do not have a target audience. I believe that there is nobody who would not be interested in this story because, you see, it is a story with elements of tragedy, thriller, action and war, psychological drama, occasionally comedy, strong emotions, big roles and epic proportions.

Christopher   Well, that certainly sounds like an evening well spent. So . . . the arrival of the Croats at the Adriatic . . .

Stribor   Kroz projekt ćemo kroz prizmu Hrvatske dotaknuti manje više cijelu povijest Europe. Jer naravno, tu su Otomansko carstvo, križarski ratovi i kletva kralja Zvonimira – ali to je, ovaj, treće poglavlje. No ukratko, tu su i Hrvatsko-Ugarska asocijacija i Pacta conventa –

Sunčana   Please – err project shows history of Europe through Croatian lens, then he lists events, Ottoman Emipre, Crusades . . .

Stribor   Austro-ugarska monarhija tzv. tamnica naroda, pa početak prvog svjetskog rata, raspad Monarhije, pa Kraljevina Srba, Hrvata i Slovenaca, pa drugi svjetski rat, pa Jugoslavija, pa Domovinski rat, pa nezavisnost, a u svemu tome sazrijevanje Europske Zajednice . . .

Sunčana   Listing more events, World Wars, Yugoslavia, the Homeland War, EU –

Astrid   Maybe if we can stick to the first chapter . . .

Stribor   Where exactly the Croats originated cannot be reliably confirmed. There are many theories, which I could now analyze for you in more detail –

Christopher   Maybe save that for the DVD extras.

Stribor   Yes. The legend says – our first . . . erm . . . kak se kaže preci . . .

Sunčana   Our first ancestors . . .

Stribor   Yes. Bili su petorica braće i dvije sestre koji su krenuli odnekuda iza Karpata, pronašli našu zemlju, evo vidite na slici, taj izraz oduševljenja kad su izbili na, je li, Jadransko more . . .

Sunčana   Were five brothers and two sisters . . . came from the Carpathians, here you see, in the painting, this expression of pure delight when they arrived at the Adriatic Sea . . .

He pauses for a moment to admire the painting.

Stribor   There they came across the Tartars –

Sunčana   Avare. Piše Avare. Avars.

Stribor   Avare, jebemti, pardon, tu se uvijek zbunim. Avars. Yes. So. They successfully defeat Avars and then seven of them create Croatia in seventh century –

Astrid   I thought you said they never invaded anyone.

Stribor   Excuse me?

Astrid   You said this was a story about a pacifist people who never fought wars of aggression.

Stribor   Šta?

Sunčana   Kaže, zar ovo nije priča o narodu pacifista koji nikad nisu vodili osvajačke ratove?

Stribor   Da, pa je. Hoću reći, mislim, nije to baš bio rat. Nego . . . pa dobro, drugo je vrijeme bilo, nekad je to bio jedini način da čovjek nađe grudu, mislim . . . al kad smo se nastanili, odonda nismo . . . mislim, nikad nismo ratovali.

Sunčana   That wasn't exactly a war. It was a different time. Since creating Croatian, we never fought wars . . .

Astrid   But you got the lands by expelling the people who lived there before you.

Stribor   Expelling? Šta, prognali? Ma nismo mi nikog prognali? Ma to je bilo neko pleme divljaka. Nisu to bili civilizirani ljudi . . .

Sunčana   It was just a tribe of savages. Not civilised people . . .

Christopher   You just said, and with more than a little glee, that these seven brothers and seven sisters –

Stribor   Two sisters. Two. Tuga and Buga . . . And the brothers Klukas, Lobelos, Koscenes, Muhlo . . . and, um, Hrvat. Yes.

Christopher   Yes, whatever, you said that Tuga and Buga and co. shipped up on the Adriatic, beat the crap out of the Avars, and thus founded Croatia.

Sunčana   Well . . . it's really only a legend. I mean, who knows what really happened. You know, an agreement of some sort . . .

Astrid   But are you proposing a historical account or a fictitious account?

Stribor   Molim te reci joj da su svi su povijesni filmovi dijelom fikcija, je li . . .

Sunčana   All historical films are at least partially fictional.

Astrid   But you said you wished to familiarise Europe with the never-before-told story of Croatia. Are you now saying it's never been told because you made it up?

Stribor   Excuse me? I made it up? What the fuck?

Astrid   There is no reason to swear.

Stribor   You say I'm a liar. You know . . . zar nije cijela povijest . . . mislim . . . all history is . . . falsifikat . . . kak se kaže –

Sunčana   Forgery –

Stribor   Forgery. Yes. But it's only little people like us, we always have to . . . nekome polagati račune . . . majku im . . .

Sunčana   Justify ourselves to others.

Astrid   Yes and now we're on the subject, you were hardly pacifist in the latest war were you?

Stribor   Šta? What do you mean by that?

Astrid   We don't need to get into that right now, but I think you know what I mean.

Stribor   And where are you from, anyway?

Astrid   That is irrelevant.

Stribor   Oh, is it really? Ova ako nije okupator, tu me reži.

Astrid   What did he say, Sunčana?

Stribor   Jeste Njemica, ha?

Sunčana   He asks if you are German.

Astrid   Yes, evidently. And what of it?

Stribor   Pa čestitam. Congratulations. German. And English, of course. No surprise there.

Astrid   We are simply pointing out some obvious weaknesses in your project. Because quite frankly, they are glaring.

Stribor   Šta kaže?

Sunčana   Da zjape rupe u projektu.

Stribor   Tko zjapi? Mama joj zjapi.

Astrid   What is he saying?

Sunčana   It's difficult to translate. There is a lot of imagery in our language.

Stribor   Da ne kažem šta joj zjapi!

Astrid Sunčana, you're not taking sides here? I mean on a national and ethnic basis? Because in this room in this place we set aside all considerations of ethnic and national nature and think as Europeans.

Christopher (*laughing*)   Always, always.

Astrid Perhaps you could assist me in this, Christopher, rather than making matters worse.

Christopher But I sort of love this project. Brilliant. Death to the Avars! Love that. The blood-myth of a people. And why not?

Astrid I should say my colleague is experiencing professional and psychological difficulties.

Sunčana Stribor is very, very passionate about this project –

Christopher Just go for it. With my blessing. I think all the little peoples of this Great Continent should have their say. I'm sure there's some Welsh performance artist somewhere wanting to have their say, I'm sure we could fund some Flems to take aim at the Walloons, and why not let the Serbs have a go when they ultimately join us.

Astrid There is no way we could possibly fund this reactionary borderline racist project.

Stribor Šta kaže?

Sunčana Ukratko, usrali smo motku.

Scene Eleven

Kobieta Mam 43 lata, mieszkam w Bydgoszczy i mam małe cycki. Wiem, że nie powinnam od tego zaczynać swojej autoprezentacji.

To jasne, że nic z tego, co powiedziałam, nie jest sexy: ani 43 lata, ani Bydgoszcz, ani cycki. Ale najbardziej te cycki. Te dzielne kobiety-feministki, które poświęciły życie, żeby mi wytłumaczyć, że nie mam obowiązku przystosowywać swojego ciała, jego niepowtarzalnej, unikalnej urody, do męskich wyobrażeń. I co? I klęska. Być może te męskie wyobrażenia o wielkich cyckach nie są prawdziwe . . . Być może są to tylko wyobrażenia magazynów life-stylowych, a mężczyźni marzą o małych piersiach, niewidocznych gołych okiem . . . Ha, ha.

Chcę tylko opowiedzieć o swoich własnych niepowtarzalnych doświadczeniach 43 lat życia z małymi cyckami. Tak, 43 lata. Bo wszystko się zmieniło w moim wyglądzie przez te 43 lata, tylko nie cycki. Wiem, są gorsze rzeczy. Ale wszystkie dziewczyny, które mają tak jak ja, wiedzą o czym mówię . . . Koleżanki skarżą się, że to takie upokarzające, kiedy facet zagląda im w dekolt. Ja wtedy kiwam głową i myślę sobie: chciałabym choć jeden raz w życiu przeżyć takie upokorzenie. Że facet zagląda mi w dekolt. Poczuć to upokorzenie całą sobą. Poczuć ten święty gniew.

1 maja 2004 roku Polska weszła do Unii Europejskiej i zaświtała mi jutrzenka nadziei. Ona się nazywała: mutacja w genie BRCA1 i BRCA2. Jest taki program unijny . . .

Scene Twelve

Szaman Premier Wielkiej Brytanii David Cameron wyciąga kartę i długo na nią patrzy. Czy jest rozczarowany? Może myślał, że duchy podsuną mu czarną panterę z „Księgi dżungli", a on wyciągnął żabę. Żabę, która przywołuje swoim śpiewem deszcz. Czy ma zacząć śpiewać i prosić o deszcz? Czy w moim kraju jest za sucho? Żaba – myśli premier – uczy szacunku do łez, ponieważ oczyszczają duszę. Kiedy ostatni raz płakałem? – pyta się w duchu. Kiedy płakał mój naród? Czy oczyścił się wtedy? Czy nadszedł czas oczyszczenia? Czemu? Czyżbym czuł się brudny? Muszę na pewien czas odłożyć wszystko – myśli premier. Muszę wziąć długą relaksującą kąpiel. Muszę wyłączyć telefon i nie wchodzić na mejla. Ale to przecież nie chodzi tylko o mnie.

Ta żaba kumka dla całego mojego kraju. Może gdzieś jest za sucho, a gdzieś za dużo błota? Może tkwimy w błocie po uszy? W śmierdzącym bagnie? Utknęliśmy tam? Może to nie jest czysty staw z liliami wodnymi? Może czas zrobić sobie przerwę, wąchać prawdziwe lilie, zjadać pyszne tłuste muchy? Kumkać? Wyłączyć umysł i kumkać?

Scene Thirteen

Kobieta   Jest taki program unijny, do którego wciągnęła mnie koleżanka.

Jest tak – jeśli odkryją u mnie mutację w genie BRCA1 o nazwie 5382insC albo mutację BRCA 1 185delIAG, ewentualnie BRCA2 6174deIT, to mi zrobią nowe cycki. Wywalą stare małe, a dadzą nowe duże – za unijne pieniądze. Bo te trzy mutacje to rak piersi w zasadzie gwarantowany. Więc jeśli odkryją te mutacje, to mam wreszcie to, o czym marzyłam, czyli poczucie bycia upokarzaną męskimi spojrzeniami.

Pomyślicie, że to jest może lekka przesada, chcieć mieć zmutowane geny? W porządku. Ja tylko chcę zapytać te, co tak się krzywią, żeby mi pokazały swój biust. Czy one wiedzą cokolwiek o życiu płaskim? Płaskim jak bezkresne stepy Rosji?

Scene Fourteen

Inozemno službeno lice   Mishal Khan was considered a bright and industrious child and showed promise in the areas of science, sport and music. He was academically the most successful of the Khan children. Although he was primarily interested in physics, a summer spent in Ulm with Indian relatives turned his attention to chemistry. After secondary school he was offered a place to study chemistry at Bristol University where he particularly excelled in the area of marine biochemistry. Shortly after graduating with distinction he obtained a position at the Institute of Chemistry and Biology of the Marine Evironment.

Ana   Mišo se ne moli ni bogu ni alahu. Kao ni ja. Jedno kratko vrijeme, rekao mi je, taman prije nego smo se upoznali, imao je neku vrstu krize identiteta pa je reklo bi se, koketirao s islamom.

Upoznali smo se 2005. U Njemačkoj. Na kongresu mladih kemičara.

U hotelu su mi dali sobu za nepušače. A ja sam imala prezentaciju drugi dan, baš sam bila nervozna i morala sam zapaliti. I tako pušim ja jednu na drugu i upali se alarm, njemački, pouzdan, naravno. Ovi iz hotela su odmah dojurili kao da sam logorsku vatru zapalila nasred sobe. Pa se ta čitava eskapada prenijela na hodnik, ja onako u pidžami, nešto vičem, bunim se protiv idiotskih propisa, malo je falilo da me daju zatvoriti. Usred skandala, izađe Mišo iz sobe preko puta i uzme me u zaštitu. Jest da je i on bio u pidžami, to ga je malo diskreditiralo kao heroja, ali me branio na impresivno tečnom njemačkom – ovi iz hotela su se smilovali i ostanem ja na slobodi. Ali sam se tako uzrujala da sam svakako morala zapaliti cigretu. Bože kad se sjetim oko čega sam se ja nekad uzrujavala. Ispostavilo se da je njegova soba za pušače i tako smo oboje u pidžamama sjedili, pušili i pili iz onih malih boca u mini-baru cijelu noć.

Oženili smo se u Zagrebu u vijećnici, onako na malo i diskretno i ja sam se preselila u Englesku. I tamo sam prvo radila kao estate agent, kak se to kaže kod nas, a onda sam se prijavila za posao u istom institutu u kojem je Mišo radio i dobila sam ga, na veliko iznenađenje. I sve je nekako bilo baš dobro.

Inozemno službeno lice   Aged twenty-eight, in 2004. Mishal Khan was briefly associated with a mosque known to the authorities as the hotbed of young Muslim radicalism in Great Britain.

This lasted a period of twelve to fourteen months after which his association with this and any other religious institution in Britain diminishes until it eventually altogehter stops.

Ana   Pošto sam ja njega provela od Dubrovnika do Varaždina, pa uključujući i Gornji Vakuf, Travnik i Sarajevo, red je bio i da ja vidim Pakistan. Taman kad smo sve organizirali, kupili karte, uzeli dopust, ispostavi se da sam trudna. Pa dobro, nije Pakistan kraj svijeta, iako se moja mama mašila za normabele čim sam joj saopćila da idemo.

I onda . . . Mobiteli nam tamo nisu radili. Pa smo dobili nečiji na posudbu. Ja sam rekla mami da ću se javljati svaki dan jer se ona bojala infekcija, toplotnog udara, proljeva, trovanja hranom, u krajnjoj liniji i terorističkih napada i da me netko uhvati da me koristi kao živi zid i svašta.

No, opsesivno sam pazila kakvu vodu pijem i prošla sam cijeli put bez problema. Obišli smo puno mjesta Karachi, Peshawar, Islamabad, gomilu rodbine, lijepo je bilo, pomalo zbunjujuće, jezik je tako težak, vruće je, a mene hormoni razvaljuju, budim se noću, trnu mi ruke, svi kažu ma to ti je normalno. Pa ne znam, nije normalno. Od svih vas dvadeset u kući, samo meni trnu ruke.

I znate što, stvarno je krasan Pakistan, a i Mišo je sav nekako tamo drugačiji. Ali ipak je on Britanac i makar nije ništa konkretno rekao, krajem trećeg tjedna, već je njemu bio pun kufer Pakistana. Baš smo se veselili da ćemo ići doma.

I nadlijećemo mi London, sav svjetlucav iz zraka, gledam Temzu kako vijuga kao zmija, a jedva sjedim više u tom malom sjedalu s trbušinom do zuba sve me boli i mislim, večeras ću biti u svojoj kupaoni, sa svim svojim stvarima, pod svojim tušem. Lijepo ću strije namazati body butterom, odjenut ću frišku spavaćicu i leći u svoj krevet, a kroz prozor će dopirati prohladan zrak i – tišina. Prvi put nakon mjesec dana, kroz prozor će se čuti tišina. I tako maštam i smješim se.

Ali u trenutku kad je policajac na carini rekao: Would you come this way, please? Mene je prošla jeza, kunem se, neka neopisiva jeza. Kao da mi London, dom i sve poznato propada pod nogama. Bez riječi objašnjenja, Mišu su odveli u drugom smjeru.

Anu oblijepe širokim selotejpom.

Scene Fifteen

Europa (*text in Croatian, German, Polish or English, it depends where is performed*)

Smeta li vam ako pušim?
Molim, govorite malo glasnije.
Što kaže?
Zapišite mi to, molim Vas.
Molim, govorite malo sporije.
Postoji li prilaz za invalide?
Jesu li psi vodiči dozvoljeni?

Da, želim postati jedna od vas, ali ako postanem jedna od vas, moram li postati ista kao vi?

Scene Sixteen

Europa   And she flees from those images that come to her in her dreams, to the shore of the ocean to look for flowers, her entourage banned among the dunes. All alone in the sunshine of a summer's day, the beautiful Europa with her heart all aflutter, breathing deeply, looks into the sun. Spots behind her eyelids – the scent of crocuses on the salty breeze: a bull approaches, iridescent, the colours kaleidoscopic – but it's no chimaera, no trick of the light.

A mighty animal – and now mingling with the sweet air there's another scent: acrid, a smell that takes her breath away and makes perspiration spring from her pores. The monster bows his extraordinary head before her, nostrils quivering – he too has sweat pouring down his shimmering rump. She touches him, feeling a pulsating under the skin of this mountain of flesh – and grabs his horns, hoisting herself up onto his back. She has no choice – this bull came to her. And now he plunges into the waves – she gives no thought to her father's sorrow when he is brought the tidings that a god has abducted his dearest daughter.

Scene Seventeen

Kobieta   Opowiadam dalej. Załapałam się do programu. Pobrali mi krew i czekałam na wynik. Nie modliłam się, żeby mieć te mutacje. Wiem, że myślicie, że Polska to katolicki kraj i my się o wszystko modlimy. Ale to nie miałoby sensu. Albo mam te mutacje, albo nie, albo mi zrobią nowy piękny biust, albo wypadam z tej zabawy.

Ale okazało się, że to jeszcze nie wszystko. Okazało się, że jeśli oni odkryją mi te 5382insC BRCA1 itd. to oznacza też, że ja, Polka-Słowianka, jestem naprawdę aszkenazyjską Żydówką – bo te mutacje występują tylko u nich. A to już, zgodzicie, się nie byle co.

Bo wy może sobie myślicie, że w Polsce to niefajnie jest być Żydem? Bo tyle tych afer było o polskich obozach koncentracyjnych i słynnym polskim antysemityzmie? Ale teraz, w 2013 roku bycie Żydem w Polsce jest kurewsko modne. Mam kolegę, który jest Żydem, i ja mu strasznie zazdroszczę. On sobie jeździ do Warszawy, do gminy reformowanej Beit Warszawa, otwartej, ekumenicznej, nie to co nasz kościół katolicki z aferami pedofilskimi, i oni mają taki fajny szabas, i to jest takie piękne . . . Bo ja tęsknię za prawdziwą duchowością . . . I ja sobie nie robię żadnych jaj w tej kwestii. U nas w Polsce, żeby znaleźć sensowny kościół, to trzeba uprawiać regularny churching. Każdy weekend w innym kościele, żeby wreszcie znaleźć coś dla siebie. Jeśli się uda, rzecz jasna.

Ale wracając do mojego kumpla, to ja mu zazdroszczę, że on tak może wzdychać ciężko. Ja wiem, że to, co teraz powiem, jest niepoprawne politycznie, ale on pójdzie sobie na cmentarz żydowski, popatrzy na te walące się menory i mówi: „oto, co zostało z kwitnącej cywilizacji" – i może się tak zasmucić, że przetrwał, że jest wyjątkowy . . . Bo my, Polacy w Polsce, wcale nie zanikamy, jest nas od chuja dużo, i ta nasza cywilizacja trwa. I nie ma się o co zasmucić, wręcz przeciwnie, jacyś tacy pospolici wydajemy się sami sobie, i ja też mam takie poczucie, że gdybym się okazała aszkenazyjską Żydówką, to bym się trochę dowartościowała.

Scene Eighteen

Ein Deutscher   Ja, und jetzt bin ich 65 und wohne noch immer in Dresden.

Europa, das war der Westen. Und Westberlin natürlich. Das kannte ich als junger Mann. Ich bin von Ostberlin dorthin gefahren, um ins Kino zu gehen, weil die Filme spannender waren. Oder zumindest zeigten, wie es dort aussieht. In Amerika. Oder in Westeuropa. Frankreich. Brigitte Bardot. Das war der Westen. Eine Frau mit Schmollmund und blonden Haaren. Ich muss das nicht weiter erklären, oder? Am Abend des zwölften August 1961 habe ich „In Freiheit dressiert" am Kurfürstendamm gesehen. Ich weiß nicht mehr, worum es da ging, ich weiß nur, dass ich am Abend wieder zurück in den Ostteil gefahren bin. Vielleicht habe ich noch ein Bier getrunken, vielleicht habe ich überlegt, noch tanzen zu gehen. Sicher ist nur, dass ich es nicht getan habe. Keine Frau kennen gelernt habe, die mich mit nach Hause nimmt. Kein gemeinsames Frühstück, leicht verlegen, in einer Schöneberger Wohnung, wortlos, weil man sich nicht kennt und lieber Radio hört, wo gesagt wird, dass Ostberlin abgeriegelt ist. Nein, das habe ich dann in meinem Studentenwohnheim in Köpenick gehört, weil ich an diesem Abend nicht abenteuerlustig war. Das war meine letzte Chance, ein Europa kennen zu lernen, das aussieht wie Brigitte Bardot.

Scene Nineteen

Mali dućan u neimenovanoj europskoj zemlji.

Dućan obiluje nacističkim obilježjima. Zastave, uniforme, fotografije i tričarije suvenirskog tipa.

Za pultom u dućanu stoji vlasnik, Svetozar. Pokazuje jedan antikni njemački šljem iz 2. svjetskog rata mušteriji neonacističke provenijencije.

Svetozar (*in a thick accent*)   Yes. This is 250 euros. I can give you for 230. I can not give you for less. Very good value.

Mušterija   Only, I saw you can get it online for 150.

Svetozar (*in a thick accent*)   150? Not possible. Only fake cost 150. Real thing 250. Because I like you English I give for 225. My last (*viče*) Željka? Kako se kaže ponuda?

Željka (*izvan scene*)   Šta je?

Svetozar   Ma, ponuda bre kako se kaže? Na engleskom?

Željka   Offer.

Svetozar (*in a thick accent*)   Offer. My last offer. Very, very good price. This antique. 1942. Very good condition.

Mušterija   OK. I'll have to think about it and come back.

Svetozar (*in a thick accent*)   OK. You think. But you cannot get better. You trust me.

Ode mušterija.

Svetozar (*ispod glasa*)   Ajd u kurac kolonijalistički. Pokrali pola planete, a nema para sad za jedan šlem.

Ulazi Željka.

Željka   Šta je bilo?

Svetozar   Ma šta bi bilo. Gleda, gleda, razgledava, ko majmun lešnik, bogati, pa sad mora da razmišlja. Evo za dvesta evra je mogao da ga dobije.

Željka   Puno je, Svetozare danas izdvojiti toliko. Nije šljem isplativ. Šta će sa šljemom? Za po doma? Vidiš da je obrijao glavu da se vidi tko je i što je i sad da ju pokrije sa šljemom.

Svetozar   Pa čekaj, pola sata me jebe! Obuko se od glave do pete u trupovsku uniformu, te daj čizmu, pa je l' broj 9, ili 9 i po il 10, nema on brate pojma evropske veličine, polomih se da mu ugodim, onda on ipak neće. Pa je l' meni na čelu piše: 'Dobričina. Zajebavaj kolko te volja.' I sad mi ti kažeš, shvati ga, nema para. Pa jesmo mi ovo iz sažaljenja radili? Ha?

Željka   Samo kažem, takva su vremena, trebamo biti solidarni. Svi smo mi u istoj kaši.

Svetozar   Ma ko je u istoj kaši? Ja s fašistima u istoj kaši? Nikad. Pa nije moj deda Bileću preživio da bih ja sad s fašistima lebac lomio. A ne, ne. U kaši istoj nismo, pa nismo. Ovo je samo biznis.

Željka   To su obični ljudi i mi smo obični ljudi. Mali obrtnici. I ti jadnici koji tu kod nas kupuju su isto svi sirotinja. Hoću reći, treba biti solidaran po toj, ekonomskoj osnovi, po kojoj smo svi najebali. Kužiš?

Svetozar   Ama, ja sam voleo da budem solidaran kad smo imali našu malu radnju. Našu Dolly Bell. Pa šta je meni falilo? Kako nam je lepo bilo nekad, Željkice, je l' se sećaš?
Željka se zamisli.

Svetozar   Kad smo se upoznali. Ti onako mlada, prognana. Žgoljavi prcvoljak, a damica. A ja bitanga. Švercer. Je l' se sećaš one naše sobice u Gete Štrase?

Željka   Sjećam se.

Svetozar   Šta li smo sve zamišljali šta ćemo i kako ćemo . . . Restoran, pa šta ti ja znam, klub za naše ljude . . . pa da dovodimo . . . Olivera i Čolu . . .

Željka   Kad je to bilo, Tozo, bit će dvadeset godina.

Oboje se zamisle.

Svetozar   A kad smo naleteli na taj lokal ?

Željka   Sjećam se . . .

Svetozar   Je l' se sećaš?

Željka   Sjećam se, sjećam. Kak se ne bi sjećala.

Svetozar   To je bila tvoja ideja. Ti si rekla, da otvorimo radnju za naše ljude. Da ne moraju više u švercu da nabavljaju Cedevitu i Vegetu i Mančmelou. Ha? Jesi tako rekla?

Željka   Kad je Cedevita najbolja kad je čovjek mamuran. A fala bogu, naši ljudi i ovdje piju ko i kod nas.

Svetozar   I više.

Željka   I više. Kad naš čovjek prvi strada. U tuđini.

Svetozar   I u tuđini i kod kuće.

Zamisle se oni. Onda se Željka prene.

Željka   Dobro, šta nama fali? Moja sestra u Zagrebu radi na minimalcu u supermarketu, duplu smjenu i ima pravo samo dvaput na zahod. Je l' ti znaš kad su joj oni dani, onda joj stave plastičnu narukvicu na ruku i onda smije češće za zahod. Pa je l' to život? Šta nama fali? Zastave idu ko alva. Jučer sam prodala dva paketa bočićnih kuglica s kukastim križem i to one retro koje su baš skupe, a Božić je tek za dva mjeseca.

Svetozar   Dobro, u pravu si, al ipak . . .

Željka   Ipak, šipak. Šuti i nadaj se da vlada neće zabraniti skup drugi tjedan. E to će nas zaviti u crno.

Svetozar   Ma. Više ne možeš nigde da kažeš šta ti je na pameti. Nema više slobode.

Željka   To si u pravu.

Svetozar   Prošla su ta vremena. Kad se setim kako nam je nekad bilo . . . Pre rata.

Željka   Je. A kolko smo se stalno nešto bunili. Ko bi si mislio šta nas čeka.

Svetozar   Da. Budale. Onakvu zemlju. U kojoj se tako fino živelo.

Željka   Dobro, vama je bilo bolje neg nama.

Svetozar   Kome?

Željka   Znaš kome. Aj, nemoj me sad potezat za jezik.

Svetozar   Jao Željka, pusti više tu priču, dosadna si i Bogu i đavolu.

Željka   Je, ja sam dosadna. Naravno. Najlakše tako.

Svetozar   Pa kad peglaš. Peglaš pa peglaš.

Željka   Dobro, ja peglam, ali istina je istina.

Svetozar   Ma koja istina?

Željka   Znaš ti dobro koja istina.

Željka   Da su svi novci išli u Beograd, ta istina. Šta misliš koja istina?

Svetozar   Pare su prvo su išle u Beograd pa su se onda ravnopravno raspoređivale.

Željka   Je, ravnopravno vama najviše pa onda na Kosovo, pa šta ostane, okrajci, to onda natrag nama. Naše vlastite pare. Mislim . . .

Svetozar   Ma ne lupaj, šta lupaš? Milion puta sam ti objašnjavao, ali kad se ti ne razumeš u ekonomiju. Takav je bio sistem – morao je neko da drži konce u rukama.

Željka   Je. Pa baš vi.

Svetozar   A ne, nego vi. Čim ste dobili priliku, odmah ste zemlju razjebali.

Željka   Mi smo zemlju razjebali?!

Svetozar   A ko je navro ko posran u potok da se otcepljuje?
Jesam ja možda?

Željka   Pa kad nam pijete krv na slamku sto godina, dobro
smo vas i trpili.

Svetozar   Željka, nemoj, pazi šta pričaš, znam ja kud ovo
ide . . .

Željka   Otpočetka. Od samog početka. Mi idealisti, a vi
zajašili.

Svetozar   E bogati, vi idealisti. E sačuvaj me bože vaših
ideala –

Željka   Hoćeš reć da nije tako? Hoćeš reć da niste imali
pretenzije otpočetka? Pa je l' nije još tvoj deda

Svetozar   Ne diraj mi dedu, heroja –

Željka   Je, heroja. Tak i mi isto danas medalje prodajemo –

Svetozar   Željka, dedu mi ne spominji, glavu ću ti razbijem,
ozbiljno ti kažem!

Željka   Dobro. Okej.

Istina. Ajde. Šta je je, je. Deda je bio heroj.

Svetozar   Bio.

Tišina.

Svetozar   Željkice . . .

Željka *šuti.*

Svetozar   Željkice.

Željka   Šta?

Svetozar   Izvini. Izvini, molim te. Kad bi ja tebe, pa znaš
ti to.

Željka   Znam.

Svetozar   Je l' znaš?

Željka   Znam.

Svetozar   Majke mi.

Željka   Ma znam!

Svetozar   Obećaj mi nešto.

Željka   Šta?

Svetozar   Obećaj mi, kad ovo sve prođe, kriza i to, obećaj mi da ćemo opet da otvorimo naš Dolly Bell.

Željka   Eh, Tozo, kad će to biti.

Svetozar   Biće, majku mu, biće. Ne može ni ovo tako unedogled.

Željka   Doći će nešto drugo.

Svetozar   Ti si nekad baš surova.

Željka   Dobro, dobro, dušo. Otvorit ćemo opet Dolly Bell. Doći će bolja vremena.

Svetozar   Evo ga, vraća se Angliz.

Željka   Vidiš. A kak si ga popljuvo.

Svetozar   A znaš mene. Brže jezik od glave –

Željka (*umiljato*)   Ma znam ja tebe.

Svetozar   Šta mogu? Zato si ti tu.

Željka   Tu sam ja. Ajde sad, ja idem pakirat hozntregere. A ti budi fin, i ne daj pički za manje od dvjesto ni pod razno. Je l' jasno?

Svetozar   Jasno. Željkice . . .

Željka   Molim?

Svetozar   Je l' me voliš?

Željka *se osmjehne.*

Scene Twenty

Ein Deutscher   Ich habe die Ausbildung beendet, geheiratet und bin nach Dresden gezogen, unser Sohn wurde geboren und im August 68 haben wir uns ein Wochenende in einer Karlsbader Pension gegönnt. Dort waren auch Westdeutsche, sie waren freundlich im Frühstücksraum. Bis sie merkten, dass wir aus dem Osten kommen. Da waren die Stühle an ihrem Tisch plötzlich nicht mehr frei. Wir wollten gerade zu einem Spaziergang aufbrechen, als der Lärm von Panzerketten zu hören war. Die Wirtin kam herein und sagte unter Tränen: Ihr seid schon wieder da, ihr marschiert schon wieder ein. Ich brauchte einen Moment, um zu begreifen, dass sie den Prager Frühling beenden. Wir gingen nach draußen und sahen die Panzer vorbeifahren, Soldaten standen auf dem Bürgersteig, um die Kolonne zu sichern. Unser Sohn fragte, was da los ist und ein russischer Soldat sagte ihm, dass der kleine Bruder in Prag krank sei und man ihm helfen müsse. Wir packten unsere Koffer und als wir das Zimmer bezahlten, flüsterte uns der Portier zu, dass die tschechischen Grenzer niemanden kontrollieren, weil alles zu chaotisch sei, jetzt könnten wir rüber gehen, morgen könne das schon wieder anders sein, wir müssten uns beeilen. Wir sind nicht gegangen und ich weiß nicht warum. Vielleicht, weil Europa an diesem Tag für mich die blasierte, übergewichtige Westdeutsche beim Frühstück war, die uns nicht an ihrem Tisch sitzen ließ.

Scene Twenty-One

Ein Deutscher   Europa auf seinem Rücken, Zeus der Allmächtige, Herrscher der Götter, Sklave seiner Lust, vielgestaltig, wenn die Jagd nach einer Frau Listen braucht um seine Lust zu stillen, an einem Ort im Westen, Kreta.

Europa   Zeus the almighty, king of the gods, slave to his desires and capable of changing shape if such cunning is required: to ensnare a woman, has Europe on his back, to satisfy his lust, somewhere in the West: Crete.

Scene Twenty-Two

Kobieta   Wiec przyszły wyniki i – wszystkie nadzieje runęły.

Owszem – znaleźli mi jedną małą mutację CHEK2 1100deIC, co oznacza zwiększoną zachorowalność na raka sutka, ale na tyle niewielką, że nic z tym nie zrobią, za to ja mam patrzeć i obserwować – jakby było na co.

No to patrzę, przez lupę, bo co mam robić, ale pomyślałam, że skoro nie jestem aszkenazyjską Żydówką, to może się więcej dowiem czegoś o swoich genach, skoro to takie łatwe. W gazecie znalazłam, że Amerykanie mają takie wielkie laboratoria genetyczne. Trzeba im zapłacić, a potem napluć w próbówkę i wysłać. I oni potem wszystko powiedzą, co wiedzą, z tej śliny, z tego, co naplute.

Okej, myślę sobie. Naplułam. Znowu czekania cztery tygodnie, ale myśl ę, raz się żyje, co sobie będę odmawiać. Jak nie jestem Żydówką, to może jakieś inne tajemnice mojego słowiańskiego genotypu się objawią.

No i przyszły te wyniki.

English actor   Your maternal Haplogroup: J2b1.

Kobieta   Tak, to właśnie ja, J2b1.

Various Actors   Haplogroup J comprising about 10–20 per cent of the populations of Iraq, Iran, Syria and Palestine, and 25 per cent of the population of the Arabian peninsula. But the haplogroup's history extends far beyond its region of origin – after the development of agriculture 10,000 years ago farmers carried offshoots of the J haplogroup from the Near East to the western fringes of Europe.

Researchers who recently disinterred the body of the fourteenth-century Italian poet Petrarch tested his mitochondrial DNA and found that it belonged to J2, a major branch of haplogroup J.

Today, J2a can be found among about 4 per cent of people living in Denmark and northern Germany. It is also found in England and parts of Scotland . . .

Kobieta   Pierwsza rzecz, którą zrobiłam, żeby coś z tego zrozumieć, to wejście na forum mojej haplogrupy J2b1. Napisałam: „Hej, jestem J2b1. Czy są tu jacyś inni J2b1?"

Various Actors   I am J2b1 and my maternal line goes back to (northeastern) Spain at the turn of the nineteenth to twentieth centuries.

I am J2b1, my maternal line is Russian (centre of Russia: Niznhy Novgorod/ Vyatka (Kirov) area. Last names: Pyankov, Blinov, Satayev.

I am also J2b1. My oldest ancestress Margaret Lynch was from Cork, Ireland and in Newport R.I. by 1860.

Hello, Iam J2b1, I'm French and my maternal line goes back to west of France since seventeenth century.

I am also J2b1. My parents are from south of Turkey. I lived in Istanbul and living both in Berlin and Istanbul now.

I am also J2b1. My earliest known ancestry goes back to England on the maternal side. Names are Holmes, Hart, Marriott, White and goes back to 1719 near Wilden in Woods, Bedfordshire, England.

I am fascinated by all your responses because most of you have European ancestry. I am also J2b1, but I am from Republic of Georgia, Mountain Jew (Google it) and my recent ancestors are from Georgia/Azerbaijan. Mountain Jews in the former Soviet Union supposedly came from Iran (via mountains), hence the name.

I am J2b1. My grandmother also used to tell me about her grandmother who was the daughter of a powerful man who went by the name of Omer Pasha (or Omer Aga), who was from the Balkans.

There don't seem to be many of us J2b1b! Here are some of my mother's ancestors – as J2b1b comes from Germany etc, I have gathered the names of the families in Germany in nineteenth century: Gobel, Zurfass, Kuhn, Stilz, Schweitzer, Botsch.

J2b1. I intuited that my distant relatives migrated from Mesopotamia through Yemen to Azerbaijan, then via raft to Finland, down to the Celtic British Isles, finally emigrating to the United States.

Scene Twenty-Three

Službeno lice   Dok su je imobilizirali samoljepivom trakom, Ana nije dospjela zatvoriti oči. Jedan kapak ostao je otvoren i priljepljen za arkadu. Tako otvoren i zaljepljen ostao je sljedećih dvadeset šest sati koliko je trajao transport na nepoznatu lokaciju.

Avionsko službeno lice   Ladies and gentlemen, we are currently flying through an area of turbulence. For your own safety please remain in your seats and fasten your seatbelts. We apologise for any inconvenience.

Službeno lice   Pomnom pretragom dokumenata prikupljenih u dosjeu Mishala Khana koji je britanska tajna služba vodila od 2003. zaključeno je da je Mishal Khan, u barem tri različite prilike, bio u vezi s terorističkim grupama koje djeluju u Velikoj Britaniji i Pakistanu. Mishal Khan u šest odvojenih navrata boravio je u njemačkom gradu Ulmu, jednom od centara islamskog radikalizma u Njemačkoj, kod rođakinje Fatime Al Usrah. Fatima Al Usrah, rodom iz Pakistana, godinama je na listi pomno promatranih njemačkih muslimana zbog velike frekvencije posjeta osoba, uglavnom muškog spola, iz Pakistana i Jordana.

Inozemno službeno lice   Combined British and Croatian intelligence suggests that Mishal Khan had on at least one occasion, on his trip to Bosnia, visited homes related to a member of a radical Muslim group, the Bosnian Vehabije. Mrs Khans's knowledge of and involvement in the matter to date remains unclear.

Aircraft official   Ladies and gentlemen, we are currently flying through an area of turbulence. For your own safety please remain in your seats and fasten your seatbelts. We apologise for any inconvenience.

Putnik 1   Mislite na osobu, ovaj, umotanu osobu? Pa je, primijetio sam, kak ne bi primijetio. Mislim, mi smo, ovoga, bili na tom letu slučajno. Mi, inače, naime, naš let je otkazan i onda je bilo pitanje da li da ostajemo još jedan dan dulje u Londonu, ili da nas stave na, ovoga, presjedanje. I ja velim Slavici, ajmo ostat, kad se već tak dogodilo. Je, ali šta? Htjeli su nas staviti u hotel na aerodromu. A to nije ko kod nas u Zagrebu da si za dvajest minuta na Jelačić placu. Tu se imaš vozit sat i pol do centra, plus to i košta, a Slavica, njoj je najgore pakiranje i raspakiravanje. Ona je jadnica jedva kofer zatvorila koliko je nakupovala. I onda smo rekli da nek nas stave na to presjedanje. Tak da mi zapravo uopće nismo ni trebali biti na tom letu. Tak da ja stvarno ne znam ni šta bih rekao. A mislim, nije red baš da se tak trudnu ženu zalijepi i da se ne može micati i . . . Ali, sad, tko zna tko je i šta je i šta je napravila. Mislim, nešto je sigurno napravila. Ali da to tako baš treba, ha, nisam pametan, šta da vam kažem. Eto. Toliko.

Putnik 2   Ne razumijem. Možda je to bila deportacija, ili performans.

Putnik 3 (*na njemačkom*)   Vidite, smatram da je to nedopustivo. Ja ipak plaćam poreze. Na kraju krajeva svi mi jako dobro znamo koliki je ogroman budžet evropskih država za nacionalnu sigurnost. Dakle, molim, ako je ta osoba već odgovorna za nešto, ili osumnjičena za neki teroristički čin, onda se takvu osobu treba transportirati na adekvatan način. A ne da se sve nas dovodi u situaciju da budemo sudionici nečega o čemu nemamo pojma i nitko nam ništa ne govori. Kakav je to način?

Putnik 4   I think it was performance art.

Putnik 5   Nemam komentara.

Putnik 6   Ja nemam komentara ali se slažem s mojim mužem.

Putnica 7   You know, it was terrible. I'll never forget it. I mean all those people pretending that nothing was happening. Awful. I mean, in whose name are they doing this? They say it's happening throughout Europe. Has anyone put this in their election manifesto, the abolishment of human rights? No, no, terrible, we should have done something.

Stjuardesa (*na njemačkom*)   Nama su samo rekli da ide s nama do Frankfurta i da joj se ne obraćamo. Je malo nezgodno. A i putnici se pitaju, a neki pitaju i mene, mislim, Bože moj, ko da sam ja neka . . . predsjednica svijeta . . . meni je samo rečeno od nadređenih, šta ja tu mogu . . .

Novinar   Judges at Europe's top human rights court will on Wednesday October fifth hear the first case to come before them arising from the US CIA's program of extraordinary rendition, the campaign of covert cross-border transfers of terror suspects, supported by a network of cross European intelligence agencies. The case has been brought by Mr and Mrs Khan, a British and Croatian citizen who were abducted by what they claim to be British agents in London in 2010 and transferred to CIA custody in a Kabul dungeon.

During the two and four months respectively they spent in captivity neither of the two were brought before the judge or charged.

Novinar 2   Mrs Khan was released a few days before her due date and flown back to Great Britain where she gave birth to a healthy baby girl on May first 2010.

Mr Khan was subsequently released having been found innocent of all allegations made against him. A compelling body of evidence corroborating Mr and Mrs Khan's story suggests that their haunting captivity was a result of no more than a case of mistaken identity.

Novinar 3   Kako doznajemo, navodi se da su već na samom početku poznanstva gospodin i gospođa Khan bili sumnjivi nadležnim organima te da je policija intervenirala u noći 21.

lipnja 2005. u njemačkom gradu Dresdenu gdje su Ana, rođena Omerpašić i Mishal Khan pokušali zapaliti hotel u kojem su odsjeli. Je li kongres mladih europskih kemičara kojeg su oboje pohađali bio samo paravan za terorističke aktivnosti, ostaje nerazjašnjeno.

Scene Twenty-Four

J2b1 Well . . . I am Greek. In case you're interested here are the results of my gene test from iGenea . . . damn this cost me $215 . . . J2b1 found in Italy, Greece, Anatolia Turkey, some Semites, and Balkans and is rumored to have ancient origin. My natural hair colour is more brownish sorta . . . I also have blue eyes. Here is a picture of me . . .

You look like you could come from any place in Europe. I would've guessed Central Europe. I don't think you look like the quintessential Greek though.

I am J2b1. My father's father's mother came from the Zidan family, which was an Arab tribe from the Galilee in Palestine. They were prominent in Tiberias, by the Sea of Galilee, and one of the patriarchs was Daher Umar Zidan, who led local insurgencies against Ottoman rule. There is a mosque in Tiberias called the Zidani mosque.

Hello, I am J2b1a2 and I am Dutch and all my female ancestors, known until 1600 were Dutch.

Kobieta Kim więc jestem? Francusko-niemiecko-holendersko-irlandzko-brytyjsko-turecko-włosko-rosyjsko-węgiersko-szkocko-gruzinsko-żydowsko-hiszpańską kobietą z małymi cyckami.

Scene Twenty-Five

Szman Premier Polski Donald Tusk wyciąga kartę z niedźwiedziem. Pierwsze, co przychodzi mu do głowy, że niedźwiedź jest lepszy od żaby, lecz wtedy słyszy głos ducha.

– Wejdź do jaskini, premierze Tusku, gdzie cisza otacza moje nauki – mówi niedźwiedź. – Pora wejrzeć we własne wnętrze, pora przetrawić doświadczenia i ustalić nowe cele.

Czy przestałem słuchać siebie? – myśli premier. Czy utraciłem moc poznania? Dlaczego mam zamęt w głowie? Gdzie się podziały moje klarowne myśli? Gdzie się podział miód życia, do którego tak bardzo tęsknię?

Premier Polski rozumie, że pora, by wszedł do Szałasu Snów. Wie, ze pora zamknąć oczy i pożegnać się z iluzją. Szałas Snów zamyka się nad nim.

Premier rusza ścieżką ciszy. Uspokaja gonitwę myśli. Teraz słucha odpowiedzi. Redaktorzy wielkich dzienników, tych z lewa i tych z prawa, wychodzą ze swoich gabinetów i wchodzą do szałasów snów. Dyrektorzy wielkich banków i korporacji, księża, biskupi, ordynariusze polowi i prymas idą za nimi. Tej nocy zamiera w Polsce życie. Każdy, kto tylko może, bierze pod łapę niedźwiedzia, przytula się do jego kosmatego futra, i zasypia, by rano wstać z odpowiedzą.

Scene Twenty-Six

Ein Deutscher   Europa, eine verpasste Liebe, die mir zweimal heimlich einen Zettel mit ihrer Adresse zugesteckt hat und ich habe mich nicht getraut, zu ihr zu gehen. Wie wäre ich empfangen worden? Wer hätte mir die Tür geöffnet?

Andere sind zu Madame Europa gefahren. In verschlossenen Zügen, die durch den Dresdener Hauptbahnhof fuhren, begleitet von Jubel und Geschrei. Ich war nicht dort. Ich war auch nicht an der Bernauerstrasse, als am 9. November die Mauer fiel. Ich war in Berlin, in der Schönhauserstrasse, in der Wohnung meines Sohnes, im Bett, mit Grippe, während er sich mit den Massen durch den Grenzübergang schob. Ich lag wach und hörte die Stadt vibrieren. Ich hätte mich aufraffen

können, ich habe es nicht getan. Ich habe Europa wieder
verpasst. – Europa – Ich habe mein Leben lang um diese
Frau geworben, keusch und ungeschickt. Ich wollte sie nicht
in einer Menge grölender Volksgenossen treffen. Nicht in
einer Kneipe, sondern in einer Sommernacht am Meer, in
einer kleinen Hafenstadt, auf deren Marktplatz eine Kapelle
spielt und festlich gekleidete Menschen unter bunten
Lichterketten tanzen. Dort werde ich Europa begegnen.

Scene Twenty-Seven

Singers   'Soave sia il vento, tranquille sia l'onda'
   'Ed ognie le mento
   Be-ni-gno ri-sponda'

Christopher   My mother used to sing it with my father.

Astrid   *Pst!*

Singers   'ai no – stride-sir.
   Soave sia il vento, tranquille la sia l'onda.'

Christopher   I've sung both the bass and the soprano line.
The room was packed, everyone stood – we were
accompanied on a piano.

Astrid   Ruhe. Das war wirklich ganz großartig.
Das Zusammenspiel von Bild und Musik ist wirklich
raffiniert. Kaffee?

Christopher *and* **Sunčana** *alone.*

Christopher   It's a bit kitschy I suppose in this form.

Sunčana   It makes me feel sick.

Christopher   Ah, but isn't beauty like that? Doesn't it
sort of upset us, reproach us? Because it makes us
think life could be better and then when it stops . . .

Sunčana   Harmony cannot occur without justice.

Christopher   Then we'd better stop making music!
Yeah, brings it all back, my first visit to Europe, with
my school, on tour, acting, all of us in this minibus, we
were young, I was young once. Performing *Hamlet* in
Elsinore, *Romeo and Juliet* in Verona, *The Merchant of
Venice*. In Venice. Completely fell for this . . . continent,
gave my life to it, even if it doesn't always . . . well –
deliver the goods.

Sunčana   You know what they should show, in their film?
They should show a Somali kid beaten blind by the Golden
Dawn. They should show a banker pissing in the eyes of a
homeless guy in London.

Christopher   No. No, that's crude, reductive.

Sunčana   They should show Moroccans sleeping in
polytunnels in Spain. Show Marine Le Pen's smile and Geert
Wilders smile and Anders Breivik –

Christopher   Now, now you're wilfully confusing the worst
with the best –

Sunčana   They should show the Danube thick with
chemicals, or an *indignado* in Madrid, or maybe a teenage
girl from Moldova trafficked into, where, Ipswich – yes,
show all these things with that music, then that would be
something to see – what do you think, Christopher?

Christopher   I tell you what I think, I think the task's
harder actually, I think we have to make the case for Europe
being something magnificent and OK, maybe we've reduced
it to bribes and bungs and trade barriers –

Sunčana   The sniffer dogs, the dying towns, the dead
currencies, the bodies in the sea.

Christopher   Oh, and the architecture, and, OK, the
prosperity – yes: fifty uninterrupted years – and the lifting
up of the Southern nations, and the re-built devastated
cities –

Sunčana   Yes, yes, the fucking Commissionaires on their High-Speed trains – the Credit Agencies flying in to write off whole nations –

Christopher   Don't we always expect too much? We always want perfection and OK, we get muddle and it is a muddle –

Sunčana   – yeah show you, and your colleagues, the political class moving from one espresso to another at your funerals in Shropshire and your sentimental shit about something that never existed.

Christopher   Look, who are you exactly?

Astrid   What – what's going on?

Christopher   Our friend here has been deceiving us.

Astrid   Sunčana?

Christopher   Is that even your name? What are you?

Sunčana   OK. Call me an artist. Say I make films, or I make events, or maybe I create . . . happenings. Say this is one right now.

Christopher   I see. And what would be the subject of this . . . happening?

Sunčana   Oh, all the big ideas. Fear. And lies. And false hope, definitely that. In fact, why not sing for us? You love Europe so much, you love culture so much, now's your chance. Sing for us.

Astrid   I'll get security.

Christopher   Don't . . . bother.

Astrid   I think you brought her in.

Christopher   Yes. That's right. All my fault, probably.

Sunčana   They'll sack you now.

Christopher   Very likely.

Sunčana   Why don't you sing then?

Christopher   Why not? Nothing to lose, nothing to be ashamed of.

Sunčana   Nothing to lose, Christopher?

Christopher, *unaccompanied, sings the bass part of 'Soave sia il vento'. He stops.*

Christopher   Happy now?

Scene Twenty-Eight

Offizier   OK. Willst du Asyl beantragen? Dann musst du nicken. Nicken. Du kannst aus dem Libanon gemäß Vertrag Dublin II bleiben, aber aufgrund der Erststaatenregelung in Griechenland. Nix Deutschland. Nix England. Nix Polen. Nix Kroatien. OK? (*Europa nickt.*)

Also, Europa, ich kann nichts versprechen. Wir müssen einfach sehen, ob wir das hinkriegen, OK? Erstmal bleibst du, Europa.

Europa   Crete, where he transforms into an eagle in order to conceive children with Europa's children who will rule Crete, where her son's son will have a bull's head: the Minotaur – not divine – misshapen, confined to a labyrinth built for him by the best of the best – grandson of Europa, roaring in the darkness, tearing human flesh in the vaults of the tremendous palace – the return of the divine as nightmare, which began so radiantly with Europa, the lady from the land of plenty.

Scene Twenty-Nine

English 1   An Englishman goes into a German pub and says to the Pole serving behind the bar . . .

German 1   Ich glaube, ich habe vergessen zu erwähnen, dass dieser Witz ohne Stereotype auskommen sollte.

English 1   You're not serious?

German 1   No stereotypes.

English 1   Would you mind if I just finish telling the joke first?

German 2   Nein, der geht auf keinen Fall. Da wird nämlich behauptet, dass Engländer saufen.

Polish 1   They are.

English 2   I'm allowed to say that. I'm English.

German 1   But Germans drink too.

English 2   That's why I said it was a German pub.

Croatian 1   Anyway, the beer tastes better in Germany.

Polish 1   What's with the Pole behind the bar? Because we only do the crap jobs?

German 1   Weil ihr nicht so unfreundlich seid wie die deutschen Bedienungen.

English 1   All right then. A German comes into an English pub and says to the Pole behind the bar . . .

German 2   Germans don't like English beer.

English 2   That's prejudice.

German 2   No, it is just an experience.

Polish 2   So wherever you go, it's still a Polish woman serving you. How come?

English 2   Realism. Have you any idea how many Poles work in the UK? Anyway I never said the Pole was a woman, that's sexist – it could be a man.

Polish 2   Unlikely.

Croatian 2   I think the joke should at least have one Croatian in it.

German 1   A Pole goes into a Yugoslavian restaurant.

Croatian 1   No such thing any more.

German 2   Aber ich habe noch nie von einem kroatischen Restaurant gehört. Habt ihr das in Polen?

Polish 1   No, definitely not. We don't even have Croatians.

English 1   What have you got in Croatia that we could put in a joke?

Croatian 1   Our government.

Croatian 1   That was a joke.

Polish 1   I think the joke should take place in Poland.

English 1   A Croatian goes into an English restaurant in Poland.

German 1   English food? Is there such a thing as English cuisine?

English 2   Curry.

German 2   We can't talk about India in a European play.

English 2   But India is the future.

Europa

Characters in order of appearance

The original production had eight actors, two from each country, but the text remains flexible and can be interpreted in any way.

Officer
Official
Europa
Sunčana
Astrid
Christopher
Shaman
Katya
Official
Ana
Stribor
Woman
Foreign Official
German
Svetozar
Customer
Željka
English Actor
Aircraft Official
Passenger 1
Passenger 2
Passenger 3
Passenger 4
Passenger 5
Passener 6
Passenger 7
Stewardess
Journalist 1
Journalist 2
Journalist 3
J2b1
Singers
English 1
German 1
German 2
Polish 1
English 2
Croatian 1
Polish 2
Croatian 2

Scene One

Officer   Right, what have we here. Unaccompanied minor with farm animal taken into custody at 7.48 am by patrol boat A 1635 off the west coast of Crete. No papers.

Official   Apparently she rode over the sea on a bull. According to the head of operations.

Officer   Do they think they're funny?

Never mind. Do we have an ID on her yet?

Official   Not yet.

Officer   Where's the bull?

Official   Down in the yard. Odd-looking kind of animal.

Officer   Right let's get on with it. Name?

Europa *doesn't answer.*

Officer   Name? All right. Me (*Points to himself.*) Diebold. (*Points to the official.*) Sikorski. (*Points to* **Europa**. **Europa** *points to herself.*)

Europa   Europa.

Officer   We got that already – destination of choice for you lot. What's your *name*?

Europa   Europa.

Officer (*wearily*)   Fetch an interpreter.

Official   Which one? We don't know where she's from, do we?

Officer   Country? State? Nation? Origin?

Europa *doesn't react – the officer fetches a map of the world, but* **Europa** *doesn't understand.*

Official   That's because Arabs don't let girls go to school.

Scene Two

The **Officer** *points to Europe on the map. Then he points to several different countries, then points at* **Europa***.*

Officer   And you?

Europa   Phoenicia.

Officer (*to the* **Official**)   You're educated, where's that then? Or is it some Lebanese tribe? They're into people trafficking. And second hand cars.

Official   I'll Google it.

Officer   What about the bull?

The **Official** *points to the horns and moos.*

Europa   Zeus.

Officer   Well that explains everything.

Official   Phoenicia used to be where Lebanon is today. Three thousand years ago.

The **Officer** *crosses something out on the form.*

Officer   Well she's hardly a minor then.

Scene Three

Sunčana *and* **Astrid**.

Astrid   Oh, are you OK with German?

Sunčana   Mein Deutsch ist nicht so gut. Englisch besser.

Astrid   So English it is. So – you found us anyway.

Your contact was Christopher?

Sunčana   That's right.

Astrid   And I think you're from Zagreb?

Sunčana   Yes.

Astrid   *Hübsche Stadt*. I lost my virginity in Zagreb.

Sunčana   Well. Congratulations!

Astrid   I have no idea why I just said that.

Astrid *laughs.*

But now you're in Brussels? Studying?

Sunčana   I gave up my studies. Money ran out.

Astrid   Well . . . *schade.*

Sunčana   Yes. I live on ten Euros a day. It is possible.

She smiles.

Astrid   So I'm Astrid, Astrid Manning – I oversee Digital and Multi-media funding Europe-wide. Christopher oversees Intercultural Dialogue.

She laughs.

Sunčana   Why, why did you laugh?

Astrid   You'll understand when you meet him.

Sunčana   And today – the money comes from – for today?

Astrid   We have a budget under-spend. I think for the last time, actually. We need to spend it or lose it; if we lose it, people ask what we are for and then we lose our jobs.

Sunčana   So you spend it on art to keep your jobs?

Astrid   Yes – no – a slightly crude account!

She checks her watch.

Where is he? OK, we will start without him.

Would you mind taking notes?

Sunčana   My pleasure.

Christopher *enters eating a waffle; he waves at everyone, takes off his coat, arranges his notes.*

Christopher   *Tut mir leid.*

Astrid   You're late.

Christopher   Had to go to a funeral, all right?

Astrid   Oh. Well. I'm sorry, of course.

Christopher   They happen a lot when you're my age. Matter of fact it was lovely; in Shropshire.

Sunčana   Shropshire?

Pause.

Should I not ask questions?

Christopher   Is this something I should know about?

Astrid   It's the intern you emailed me about.

Christopher   Intern? I sent no such email.

Sunčana   I sent you my CV. Sunčana, hi.

Christopher   Right. You're sure of that?

Sunčana   Every day since I have emailed you.

Christopher   Yes, yes of course. The . . . Slovenian?

Sunčana   Croatian.

Christopher   My mistake.

Astrid   As we've had secretarial support cut it's fortunate she's here.

Christopher   *Ausgezeichnet*. Unpaid labour. Definitely the future of Europe.

Astrid   So maybe we can get going?

Christopher   Great to finally meet you Sun . . . cana.

Sunčana   Sunčana.

Christopher   'Sunčana' – yes, I was in Shropshire, yes, for a funeral.

Sunčana   Who died?

Christopher   Oh. My mother, actually.

Sunčana   I'm sorry.

Christopher   Don't be. It was . . . a kindness.

Yes, a beautiful event – she was a Humanist, these things can be quite embarrassing but I read some Goethe, we sang that aria from 'Cosi' – you know – 'Soave sia il vento'. Corny perhaps, but . . . very moving.

Scene Four

Shaman   The biggest tragedy of Europe is the fact that it stopped believing in ghosts. Europe laughed out its ghosts and forgot them.

Europe is deaf.

It cannot hear any ghosts – ghosts of water and air, ghosts of Earth, ghosts of crocuses, bulls and chimaeras.

Europe does not have to listen to me either. It will not put me off. It is my duty to remind it about ghosts.

I want it to consider a completely different form of making common decisions. I would like Europe, with its leaders, to meet in a big circle where there are no important or less important ones.

I would like the leaders to ask questions, ask questions about the future of each country, them, not the political advisers, ministers of finances, European Parliament; other people and institutions of that kind.

I would like them to ask ghosts all the questions.

Scene Five

Astrid   If you don't feel up to this –

Christopher   What could be more of a tonic than meeting a bunch of artists?

Astrid   Sunčana, would you mind fetching in the first applicant? Thank you.

Sunčana *brings in* **Katya** *comes before them.*

Astrid   Katya. Live artist.

Sunčana   From Kuressaare, Estonia.

Katya   Yes. Hello!

Kuressaare. Yes.

Astrid   Hello Katya.

Thanks for coming all this way. So, if you can, briefly detail your proposal, that would be brilliant.

Katya   OK. In Englisch?

Christopher *laughs.*

Astrid   English is fine.

Katya   Title: 'Fire Sale'. You receive details?

Astrid   We'd like to hear a bit more from you, the artist – and I should say, we are seeing a lot of people today so brief is great.

Katya   OK. OK.

Katya *pulls a lighter out of her pocket.*

Christopher   What's she doing?

Astrid   No idea.

Now she pulls out a ten Euro note.

Katya   OK. Ten Euro note. So.

Astrid   OK, yes, we got that.

Now she ignites the lighter and sets the note alight.

Christopher   Actually, we have a smoke alarm in here. A very sensitive smoke alarm, notoriously hard to disable.

The smoke alarm goes off.

Astrid   You really need to stop burning things.

Sunčana   Are these real euros?

Katya   I make . . . 'pyre' – 'pyre'?

Christopher   Absurdly over-reactive.

Astrid   The criteria for the awards, the grants are largely based on 'Intercultural Dialogue', or, err, 'Embodiment of European Spirit' –

Katya   Excuse me, this is, this is better: 'FIRE-SALE – title – Europe: common denominator: MONEY'! Burn – dying currency, in burning, allow to be re-born? OK?

Astrid   OK, thank you, Katya.

We need to stop it there. I think.

Katya   Is all?

Astrid   We have your portfolio.

Katya   I come a long way.

Christopher   We cover expenses I think.

Katya   OK. OK. Bye, bye.

Hope you like 'Fire Sale'.

Scene Six

Shaman   I repeat: I would like the leaders to ask questions, ask questions about the future of each country, then, not the political advisers, ministers of finances, European Parliament; other people and institutions of that kind. I would like them to ask ghosts at the questioner.

Everyone, for instance Angela Merkel, the Chancellor of Germany, would have the opportunity to ask ghosts of animals, what is, they think her or his country needs.

And there, Angela Merkel, concentrated and peaceful, raises her left hand and gently passes it over the Cards of Healing Power out of which one will answer the question about Germany's role in the common Europe. Angela Merkel picks a coyote. She looks at it for a while and thanks him. Who is the coyote?

Angela Merkel comes back to the circle with an image of the coyote in her heart. From that moment on, many aspects of the coyote's power will be discussed in the country's media. What does the card mean? Moral authorities, philosophers, scientists will start wondering together what kind of lesson coyote offers to Germany.

Coyote, a jester, a looney and a trickster. Maybe Germany's trouble is too much of seriousness? There are so many things one can laugh about, but nobody does, everyone is serious. Why has Germany stopped laughing? Why have they stopped playing around? Why is it so difficult to look at a situation from a different perspective than with all that seriousness? What is the heavy stuff that Germany carries along? These are the questions Angela Merkel is now asking herself. She also wonders, when has she stopped laughing at herself? It is all far too serious. Where have jokes and laughter gone? Why shouldn't she play a trick? How about telling Hollande, with a serious face, that I like to pole-dance in my free time? Or that at nights I draw moustaches on the faces of women from billboards promoting washing powders?

These are Chancellor's private thoughts, but she also thinks about the whole country. When did it happen, all the seriousness? Dead seriousness? Does Germany really need to be so serious all the time? Do we always need to be so responsible?

Nobody thinks we can be crazy. Why did we become prisoners of such a serious image? Perhaps it is not a sad image, but it is stiff. Boring. Why have we become the most boring people in Europe? Rich, boring people. What do we need it for? Are we happy about it? Why does everyone expect Germany to be so responsible? Is it pleasant to always be the responsible ones? If we are the responsible ones, then somebody else will be the one who is always irresponsible, There is no balance then. This is no good.

Angela Merkel looks at the leaders of the other countries and she can see in their eyes that unless she stops being so responsible, the others will always be irresponsible. And she can see they start to understand that if Germany picked the coyote, then something needs to change.

And the change will come. Now Germany will take over the leadership in laughter, fun and joy. 'Cause this situation cannot last any longer. 'Cause they are tired. They slouch with a torment of seriousness on their faces. It is no fun. It is not right. And it is not fair to Germany.

Scene Seven

Official   Ana Esma Khan was born in Zagreb in 1979 to father Munir and mother Marijana. Her parents met at the Faculty of Politics in the mid-1970s. Her father, Munir Omerpašić, Mujo to his friends, was born in Gornji Vakuf and moved to Zagreb in 1975. He met Marijana Tot-Hladika during his second year at university and their relationship soon resulted in marriage when Marijana was three months pregnant with Ana's older brother Tarik. Ana Esma Omerpašić, born two years later, was named after her grandmother Ana Tot at her mother's insistence. Her brother Tarik had inherited his great-grandfather's famous name. There is a legend in the Omerpašić family that their lineage extends all the way back to Mehmed-beg of Stolac, the founder of Gornji Vakuf, but there is little actual evidence to support this theory, which was often the subject of arguments between the married couple.

Ana   Mum always thought Dad was a bit of a peasant. Like all his family, even if they were the noblest of Bosnian nobility. However, whenever someone else dared say anything on the subject of Dad's common Bosnian origins, Mum would leap like a lioness to his defence. This was usually my grandmother who claimed to have some distant noble Hungarian origins herself but the evidence to support this claim was purely arbitrary.

Mum always used to tell us, my brother and me, about the great Muslim contributions to our civilisation and about their rich culture about which we learned nothing at school.

Neither Mum nor Dad prayed to God or Allah. Religion-based arguments arose very occasionally, usually during Sunday lunch when Granny decided to elaborate on how we Croats had always been the ramparts of Christianity and how as far back as the 15th century our old friend the Pope had named us Antemurale Christianitatem And if it hadn't been for us, 'The Turks would have overrun us and today the whole of Europe would bow to the East five times a day.'

Then Dad would say Granny was just an upstart, and anyway it wasn't Antemurale Christianitatem, but Christianitatis, as it was the genitive case.

But generally, my father Munir, mother Marijana, brother Tarik and I, Ana, we were all Yugoslavs.

Foreign Official   Mishal Khan was born in 1976, in Birmigham. His grandfather Malik Khan fought for the British Indian Army during the British Raj but it wasn't until 1954 that Mishal's father Hassan and his wife Saaida moved to the West Midlands. Mishal's father was a doctor and his mother a housewife. After settling in Great Britain they raised four children. Mishal, Fatima, Ahmed and Sanjiv.

Ana   My mother was not happy when I met Mišo. 'You and your Muslim gene, you're a Zagreb girl and of all the men in the world, you manage to fall for this one. He's not even one of our Muslims. No, he's the real thing. Look at him, it's just as well you don't have any sun in England. Couple hours in the sunshine he'd change five shades before your eyes.'

All her life Mum worried that I'd fall in love with someone from a country where women don't have the vote, who'd drag me away to his family like that woman from *Not Without my Daughter*. So when I met Mišo, Mum had a nervous breakdown. And even Dad was a bit sceptical. 'You know, we're Europeans, mouse, and they're something different.' So said my father Munir who has called me mouse[1] all my life which resulted in various misunderstandings when Mishal joined our family. Mishal, who was born in Great Britain.

True, the British don't particularly think of themselves as Europeans, but Mišo certainly thinks that he's the heir to the achievements of Western civilisation more than my father Munir from Gornji Vakuf is. They'll probably remain suspicious of each other all their lives.

But in fact, when she finally met him, my mother immediately fell for Misho. She and Misho both speak excellent German and love literature, Indian in particular. They spend hours dissecting Rushdie and Kureishi in German which makes my mum feel really important. Because my father Munir, apart from history books, only likes Andrić and Jergović. He used to like Aralica as well, but that love came to an end some years ago.

But my Mišo, he can read for days on end. He is always reading books about Pakistan and India. He feels a constant need to understand himself and his family, who they were and what they belong to. Being Yugoslavian first and then becoming Croatian was confusing enough for me. But to be a Pakistani in Britain . . . nowadays . . . to feel a sense of belonging to both identities . . . I think Mišo's a hero. I think that's why I fell for him. Something's always in flux inside him.

---

[1] Croatian word for mouse is miš (pronounced mish). Mišo, short for Mihael or Mišel is also a male name or a term of endearment

Scene Eight

Europa   Europa – daughter of the king who lent his country its name, Phoenicia. Phoenicia: birthplace of money and territory of traders, whose ships sailed as far as the pillars of Hercules to exchange their wares – weighed in gold – in the palaces of her childhood: a golden youth, the most beautiful of beauties, proud and headstrong – the only one allowed to answer her father Phoenix back: her adoring father, Europa the apple of his eye, able to wind him round her little finger. Her only knowledge of men being those bowed backs at her father's court and the adulating tones of the Eunuchs: her wish their command, their very lives at the mercy of her tempestuous moods.

Scene Nine

Shaman   Croatia's Prime Minister, Zoran Milanovic, picks a card with an elk, and he shivers. The elk is the essence of self-esteem. It is his power – the elk's power. What happened to elk's roar? Why is it not heard in the European forest? Why is it quiet? Where is its voice? Where is the voice of a proud king of the forest who has done so much and announces it with a roar? – Croatian Prime Minister wonders. Where did our self-esteem go? Where is the pride of our nation? What happened to it? Where did the pride of our experience go? The wisdom of elk is the wisdom of an experienced warrior, who travelled for a long time, who fought, who saw a lot and did a lot and he has already become a member of the elders.

Now he takes joy in preaching, he shares his wisdom with others. Perhaps I stopped thinking of myself as a wise man? – Croatian Prime Minister wonders. Perhaps all the Croatian people stopped considering themselves as wise people, maybe they think that other nations know better? The elk knows when it is time to roar. Is this what is happening? – Prime Minister wonders. Do we know when we should roar proudly? Do we respect our experience and share it?

Do we praise and warn? Are we surrounded by respect? Do they ask for our opinion during conferences? Our wisdom is great, greater than other members of the circle might think. Now they look at the card picked by Croatia and wonder what does this mean for them? Maybe they have only attributed the privilege of wisdom to themselves? And the ceremony of the circle shows something different. Perhaps all should think this through.

Scene Ten

All dialogue set in bold is spoken in Croatian.

Culture programme – **Stribor** *is setting up a presentation – the title in Croatian and English – The Stone is Burning the Wave is Frothing (*Kamen gori val se pjeni*).*

Astrid   Sunčana, can this fellow speak English?

Sunčana   Stribor has prepared the whole presentation for you in English in this folder.

Christopher   Do we even fund Croatian art yet? I mean are they on-stream?

Astrid   If it makes a positive contribution to European culture which I am sure –

Stribor   **What is she saying** – we are not a positive contribution? What is she saying –

Sunčana   It's best you focus on the presentation. On being clear and concise.

Christopher   Looks fiendishly complex.

Stribor   Yes. I am aware. But that's exactly what I think is necessary. **The multimedia project The Stone is Burning the Wave is Frothing will be the most comprehensive performance project about the history of the Croatian people to date. We in Tuga i Buga Productions believe that the time is absolutely right for such a project.**

Sunčana 'The Stone is Burning the Wave is Frothing . . .' intended to be the biggest project telling history of Croatian people, never been tried before . . .

Stribor The theme of this project is also the reason why it has not been done yet – that is the unreliability of sources throughout our history under foreign rule leading to the impossibility of understanding our own identity.

Sunčana . . . he even says the theme of this project is in fact why it is being done . . . err – unreliability . . .

Stribor . . . Uneraliabilty, yes . . .

Sunčana . . . of historical record which was in the hands of occupying powers making it impossible for us to understand our own identity.

The board members look through their papers searching for a simpler explanation.

Stribor Maybe it is not good for Europe to bring into its . . . so to speak . . . organism . . . an . . . organ which it does not know. What is particularly specific about Croats as such is that they are one of the few nations, you could even say among the only nations in Europe who have never waged wars of aggression.

Sunčana What is particularly specific about Croats as such is that they are among the rare nations in Europe, maybe the only one, who have never waged wars of aggression.

Astrid Ach, das wusste ich nicht. Interessant.

Sunčana Stribor has apparently prepared a video presentation as a kind of a guide through the chapters of history.

A film starts to run with images of beaches on the Croatian coast and women in swimming costumes. Here is even Ana Sasso, emerging out of the water. There are also images of suntanned young men in swimming trunks.

Stribor   I am sorry. This is another presentation.

Stribor *fiddles with the laptop.*

The first chapter – seventh century AD, captured in this famous painting by Oton Ivekovic . . .

Sunčana   Beginning of project shows arrival of Croats in country as shown in famous painting by Oton Ivekovic.

Stribor   Arrival of the Croats at the Adriatic . . .

The painting appears on the screen.

Astrid   Can he tell us anything about his target audience?

Stribor   No, sorry, I do not have a target audience. I believe that there is nobody who would not be interested in this story because, you see, it is a story with elements of tragedy, thriller, action and war, psychological drama, occasionally comedy, strong emotions, big roles and epic proportions.

Christopher   Well, that certainly sounds like an evening well spent. So . . . the arrival of the Croats at the Adriatic . . .

Stribor   Through the Croatian prism we are going to address more or less the whole of European history. The Ottoman empire, the Crusades and the curse of King Zvonimir, which is, err, the third chapter. But, to make a long story short, Croatian-Hungarian Association, Pacta conventa . . .

Sunčana   Please – err project shows history of Europe through Croatian lens, then he lists events, Ottoman Emipre, Crusades . . .

Stribor   Austro-Hungarian Monarchy, the so called dungeon of the people, World War I, the collapse of the Monarchy, the Kingdom of Serbs, Croats and the Slovenes, World War II, Yugoslavia, Homeland War, independence, and alongside all of this the maturing of the European Union . . .

Sunčana   Listing more events, World Wars. Serbian rule, Yugoslavia, the Homeland War, EU –

Astrid   Maybe if we can stick to the first chapter . . .

Stribor   Where exactly the Croats originated cannot be reliably confirmed. There are many theories, which I could now analyse for you in more detail –

Christopher   Maybe save that for the DVD extras.

Stribor   Yes. The legend says – our first . . . erm . . . ancestors . . .

Sunčana   Our first ancestors . . .

Stribor   Yes. Our first known ancestors, legend has it, were five brothers and two sisters who started their journey somewhere behind the Carpathians, found our country, here you see, in the painting, this expression of pure delight when they arrived at the Adriatic Sea . . . Jadransko more . . .

Sunčana   Were five brothers and two sisters . . . came from the Carpathians, here you see, in the painting, this expression of pure delight when they arrived at the Adriatic Sea . . .

He pauses for a moment to admire the painting.

Stribor   There they came across the Tartars –

Sunčana   Avars. It says here Avars.

Stribor   Avars, shit, I always get mixed up here. Avars. Yes. So. They successfully defeat Avars and then seven of them create Croatia in seventh century –

Astrid   I thought you said they never invaded anyone.

Stribor   Excuse me?

Astrid   You said this was a story about a pacifist people who never fought wars of aggression.

Stribor   What?

Sunčana   She says, isn't this supposed to be a story of a pacifist people who never fought invading war.

Stribor   Well . . . we haven't. I mean, that wasn't exactly a war. But . . . well OK, it was a different time, then it was the only way for a man to find his own piece of land, I mean . . . once we'd established our country, after that we didn't . . .

Sunčana   That wasn't exactly a war. It was a different time. Since creating Croatian, we never fought wars . . .

Astrid   But you got the lands by expelling the people who lived there before you.

Stribor   Expelling? What? We didn't expel anybody. They were just a bunch of savages –

Sunčana   It was just a tribe of savages. Not civilised people . . .

Christopher   You just said, and with more than a little glee, that these seven brothers and seven sisters –

Stribor   Two sisters. Two. Tuga and Buga . . . And the brothers Klukas, Lobelos, Koscenes, Muhlo . . . and, um, Hrvat. Yes.

Christopher   Yes, whatever, you said that Tuga and Buga and co. shipped up on the Adriatic, beat the crap out of the Avars, and thus founded Croatia.

Sunčana   Well . . . it's really only a legend. I mean, who knows what really happened. You know, an agreement of some sort . . .

Astrid   But are you proposing a historical account or a fictitious account?

Stribor   Please tell her, all historical films are partly fictional . . .

Sunčana   All historical films are at least partially fictional.

Astrid   But you said you wished to familiarise Europe with the never-before-told story of Croatia. Are you now saying it's never been told because you made it up?

Stribor   Excuse me? I made it up? What the fuck?

Astrid   There is no reason to swear.

Stribor   You say I'm a liar. You know . . . isn't all of history . . . I mean . . . all history is . . . **forgery, what you call it . . .**

Sunčana   Forgery –

Stribor   Forgery. Yes. But it's only little people like us, **we always have to . . . lay accounts to others . . . fucking . . .**

Sunčana   Justify ourselves to others.

Astrid   Yes and now we're on the subject, you were hardly pacifist in the latest war were you?

Stribor   **What**? What do you mean by that?

Astrid   We don't need to get into that right now, but I think you know what I mean.

Stribor   And where are you from, anyway?

Astrid   That is irrelevant.

Stribor   Oh, is it really? (*To* **Sunčana**.) **I'll be damned if she's not from 'the Occupiying forces'.**

Astrid   What did he say, Sunčana?

Stribor   **Are you German?**

Sunčana   He asks if you are German.

Astrid   Yes, evidently. And what of it?

Stribor   Congratulations. (*He looks at their name-plates.*) German. And English, of course. **No surprise there.**

Astrid   We are simply pointing out some obvious weaknesses in your project. Because quite frankly, they are glaring.

Stribor   What's she saying?

Sunčana   That you have glaring holes in the project.

Stribor   The what? Her momma's glaring . . .

Astrid   What is he saying?

Sunčana   It's difficult to translate. There is a lot of imagery in our language.

Stribor   And it's not the only thing on her glaring.

Astrid   Sunčana, you're not taking sides here? I mean on a national and ethnic basis? Because in this room in this place we set aside all considerations of ethnic and national nature and think as Europeans.

Christopher (*laughing*)   Always, always.

Astrid   Perhaps you could assist me in this, Christopher, rather than making matters worse.

Christopher   But I sort of love this project. Brilliant. Death to the Avars! Love that. The blood-myth of a people. And why not?

Astrid   I should say my colleague is experiencing professional and psychological difficulties.

Sunčana   Stribor is very, very passionate about this project –

Christopher   Just go for it. With my blessing. I think all the little peoples of this Great Continent should have their say. I'm sure there's some Welsh performance artist somewhere wanting to have their say, I'm sure we could fund some Flems to take aim at the Walloons, and why not let the Serbs have a go when they ultimately join us.

Astrid   There is no way we could possibly fund this reactionary borderline racist project.

Stribor   What now?

Sunčana   In a nutshell, you've blown it.

Scene Eleven

Woman   I am forty-three years-old, live in Bydgoszcz and I have got small tits. I know I should not be starting my auto-presentation with that. It is quite obvious, that none of these things – nor being forty-three, nor Bydgoszcz or small tits are sexy. But the tits. . . tits are the worst. As if it was not enough, I feel guilty saying this. All the brave women – feminists, who devoted their lives to explain it to me, that I am not obliged to adjust my body, its one and unique beauty to men's repreimagination. And . . .? Defeat. Perhaps these men's imaginations about big boobs are not real? Perhaps these are only imaginations of the life-style magazines, and men dream of small breasts, not visible to the naked eye. Ha, ha.

I only want to tell about my own, unique experience of having lived forty-three years, and having small boobs all that time. Yes, forty-three years. 'Cause everything in my looks has changed throughout those years, everything but the breasts. I do know there are worse things. But all the girls who share this problem know what I mean . . . When friends complain on how very humiliating it is having a guy staring at their cleavage, I nod my head thinking: 'I wish I had that one and only time of such a humiliation in my life: a man staring at my cleavage.' To feel the humiliation with my whole body and mind. To feel the sacred anger.

First of May 2004 Poland accessed the European Union and I felt there was hope for me. It was called: mutation in BRCA1 and BRCA2 genes.

There is a EU programme . . .

Scene Twelve

Shaman   Prime Minister of Great Britain David Cameron picks a card and stares at it for a long time. Is he disappointed? Perhaps he thought that ghosts would chose for him the black panther from *The Jungle Book*? And he picked a frog that calls for rain with its song. Should he start singing and asking for rain? A frog – Prime Minister thinks, it teaches respect for tears because they clean the soul. When was the last time I cried? – he wonders. When was the last time my nation cried? Did they heal then? What was happening at that time?

Why should I sing and ask for rain? Is it too dry in my country? Is it time for a catharsis? Why? Is it possibe that I feel dirty? Tired? Tormented? Frustrated? Nervous? Weakened? Lost?

Maybe I should postpone some things for a while – the Prime Minister wonders. I must take a long, relaxing bath. I must switch off my phone and must not check my mailbox. I must tell myself: 'Enough'. I must breathe deeply. But it is not only about me. The frog croaks for my whole country. Perhaps it is too dry somewhere, and perhaps there is too much mud somewhere else? Maybe we are all covered in mud? We are stuck in a stinky swamp? Maybe it is not a clean pond with water lillies? Maybe we overwhelmed ourselves and it is time for rest? Maybe it is time to take a break, to smell real lillies, to eat delicious, fat flies? To croak? Pray for rain? Turn off our minds and simply croak?

Scene Thirteen

Woman   There is a EU programme to the participation of which my friend talked me into. It goes: if they discover a mutation 5382insC or BRCA 1 185delAG, or, at least BRCA2 6174deIT of my gene, then I will get a boob job. They will take out the old, small tits and give me brand new, big ones – for European money. The thing is, that these three kinds of mutation, give you breast cancer, guaranteed. So, if they discover the mutation, then I have what I dreamt of: feeling of humiliation caused by men's glances.

You may think this is all exaggerated, wanting to have my genes mutated, okay. I just wanna ask all the gals who moan, to show me their breasts. Do they know anything about life on a plain? Plain as flat as boundless Russian steppes?

Scene Fourteen

Foreign Official   Mishal Khan was considered a bright and industrious child and showed promise in the areas of science, sport and music. He was academically the most successful of the Khan children. Although he was primarily interested in physics, a summer spent in Ulm with Indian relatives turned his attention to chemistry. After secondary school he was offered a place to study chemistry at Bristol University where he particularly excelled in the area of marine biochemistry. Shortly after graduating with distinction he obtained a position at the Institute of Chemistry and Biology of the Marine Evironment.

Ana   Mišo doesn't pray to God or Allah. The same as me. Just before we met, he told me, he did have a sort of an identity crisis, briefly flirted with Islam, for want of a better word.

We met in Germany in 2005. At a chemists' convention.

They gave me a non-smoking room. I had a presentation the next day and was really nervous so I had to light up. I smoked one after the other and set off the predictably reliable German smoke alarm. The hotel people appeared within seconds – you'd think I lit a bonfire in the middle of the room. The whole episode moved out into the corridor where I proceeded to protest against the idiotic rules and almost got myself arrested. Wearing pyjamas. I mean! Mišo was in the room opposite and came to my defence. OK, so the hero role was somewhat diminished by the fact he too was wearing pyjamas. But he defended me in fluent German, which was quite impressive and so they showed mercy and I kept my freedom. But I was so upset (I mean the things I used to get upset about, my God) I just had to light a cigarette. It turned out he had a smoking room so he invited me over for a cigarette and a drink and we stayed up all night, in our pyjamas, smoking and drinking from those tiny bottles in the mini-bar.

We spent the first few years travelling back and forth, and even once went on a tour of ex-Yugoslavia. We visited Vakuf and dad's relatives, who again boasted about their noble origins, my mother kept rolling her eyes until a standard row ensued.

Then we decided to get married. We had a ceremony in a registry office in Zagreb, a small discreet affair, and then I moved to England. My first job in England was as an estate agent and then I got a job at the same Institute where Mišo worked. Things were going well.

Foreign Official   Aged twenty-eight, in 2004. Mishal Khan was briefly associated with a mosque known to the authorities as the hotbed of young Muslim radicalism in Great Britain.

This lasted for a period of twelve to fourteen months after which his association with this and any other religious institution in Britain diminishes until it eventually altogehter stops.

Ana   Then we decided to visit Pakistan. As I had dragged him from Dubrovnik to Varaždin, even taking in Gornji Vakuf, Travnik and Sarajevo, it was now my turn to see Pakistan. And just when we'd got everything organised, bought the tickets, booked our holidays, I found out I was pregnant.

Well, Pakistan is not the end of the world, is it, there are plenty of pregnant women there too. Nonetheless, my mother started taking Xanax the moment I told her we were going.

And then when we got there . . . first we couldn't get our mobile phones to work. So we borrowed an old used one from one of the relatives. I had to check in with my mother all the time as she was afraid of infections, heatstroke, diarrhoea, food poisoning and even terrorist attacks, or that I get used as a human shield or something.

Anyway, I paid obsessive attention to water and experienced no problems. We got to see a lot of Pakistan, Karachi, Peshawar, Islamabad, a tone of family . . . It was wonderful, intense, somewhat confusing . . . I barely speak the language and my hormones are driving me crazy. I wake up, middle of the night, with pins and needles in my arms. Everyone keeps telling me not to worry, that's perfectly natural. Certainly easy to say, but I'm the only one out of twenty in the house waking up every night with pins and needles.

And you know, Pakistan really is beautiful, and Mišo is a different man there. It brings out something wonderful in him. But ultimately he really is British. My grandmother Zeina and my great-grandmother Aisha make me a better fit for all of them than him with his 'stand-behind-the-yellow-line' take on the world. He didn't say it in so many words, but by the end of the third week he'd already had enough of Pakistan. We were happy to be going home.

So we're flying into London. The journey is so long and I can barely fit into the seat with my massive belly . . . We're flying over London, so beautiful and twinkly from high up. I see the Thames, crawling like a snake through the city and I say to myself, I'll be in my own bathroom tonight. I'll be in my own shower, I'll rub body butter over my strech-marks, I'll sleep in my bed in fresh sheets by an open window. Outside there will be a cold night breeze and I'll be able to hear silence . . . For the first time in a month I'll hear silence through the window.

But the moment the man said: 'Would you come this way, please?' a shiver ran through me. I swear, a horrible shiver.

As if London, home and everything familiar were dissolving under my feet. Mišo was led away in the opposite direction.

Several men in indeterminate uniforms seize **Ana**.

Ana *struggles.*

They wrap **Ana** *from head to toe in wide adhesive tape.*

Scene Fifteen

Europa (*text in Croatian, German, Polish or English, it depends where is performed*)

Do you mind if I smoke?
Can you speak up, please?
What is she saying?
Can you write that down, please?
Please, speak more slowly.
Is there a wheelchair approach?
Are the guide dogs allowed?

Yes, I would like to be one of you, but if I become one of you will I have to become the same as you?

Scene Sixteen

Europa   And she flees from those images that come to her in her dreams, to the shore of the ocean to look for flowers, her entourage banned among the dunes. All alone in the sunshine of a summer's day, the beautiful Europa with her heart all aflutter, breathing deeply, looks into the sun. Spots behind her eyelids – the scent of crocuses on the salty breeze: a bull approaches, iridescent, the colours kaleidoscopic – but it's no chimaera, no trick of the light.

A mighty animal – and now mingling with the sweet air there's another scent: acrid, a smell that takes her breath away and makes perspiration spring from her pores. The monster bows his extraordinary head before her, nostrils quivering – he too has sweat pouring down his shimmering rump. She touches him, feeling a pulsating under the skin of this mountain of flesh – and grabs his horns, hoisting herself up onto his back. She has no choice – this bull came to her. And now he plunges into the waves – she is deaf to the cries of her servants, who know that her life is forfeit; she gives no thought to her father's sorrow when he is brought the tidings that a god has abducted his dearest daughter.

Scene Seventeen

Woman   Anyway. I was chosen for the programme. They took my blood and so I waited for the results. I was not praying to have this mutation. I know you think that Poland is a Catholic country, and we pray for all kinds of things. But it would not make sense. Either I have the mutation, or I have not, either I have my new, beautiful breasts, or I am out of this game.

However, it turned out that was not the whole story. What started with dreams about big boobs, turned out to be the fact: if they really discover all the 5382insC etc. that means that I – Polish, Slavic woman am really an Ashkenazi Jewish woman – 'cause they always have this kind of mutation.

And you will agree this is quite a thing. Maybe you think being a Jew in Poland is not such a nice thing? Because of all the mess with 'Polish concentration camps' and the famous Polish anti-Semitism? Now, in 2013 it is whole lotta different. Nowadays being Jewish in Poland is fucking awesome!

I have a friend who is Jewish, and I envy him so much.

He goes to Warsaw, to 'Beit Warsaw' – open, ecumenical, not like our Catholic church with all the paedophile scandals, and they have there a 'shabbat', so cool, and this is so beautiful . . . 'Cause I miss genuine spirituality . . . And this is no joke. Here, in Poland, to find a nice, decent church you need to go 'churching' regularly – each weekend in a different church, to find something for oneself. If you succeed, of course.

Coming back to my friend, I envy him about how deeply can he sigh. I realise that what I will say right now is politically incorrect, but he can always go to a Jewish cemetery, look at the ruined menorahs and say: 'This is all that was left of the flourishing civilisation' – and he can be sad, thinking he survived, thinking he is unique . . . We, Polish people in Poland, do not fade at all, there is a fucking lot of us, and our civilisation abides. And there is nothing to be sad about, on the contrary, we all seem so average to ourselves, common, and I feel that if it turns out that I am an Ashkenazi Jewish woman, I would get some self-confidence.

Scene Eighteen

German Europe. That meant the West. And West Berlin of course. That's how it was when I was young. I used to go there from East Berlin to go to the cinema. The films were more exciting there. Or at least to see what it looked like over there. In America. Or in Western Europe. France. Brigitte Bardot. That was the West. A blonde with a pout. Need I say more? On the evening of the twelfth of August 1961 I saw *Please, Not Now!* on the Kufürstendamm. I don't remember what it was about – all I know is that I went back to the East that night. Maybe I had another beer, maybe I thought about going to a club. The only thing I know now is that I didn't in the end. Didn't meet a woman who took me back to hers. Didn't have breakfast with her listening to the radio with nothing to say because you didn't really know each other. Didn't therefore hear the announcement that the border to East Berlin had been sealed. No, I found it out in my student place in Köpenick, because on that particular evening I hadn't felt particularly adventurous. That was my last chance to get to know a Europe that looked like Brigitte Bardot.

Scene Nineteen

A small shop in an unnamed European country. The shop is crammed full of Nazi memorabilia: flags, uniforms, photographs and small souvenirs. The owner, **Svetozar***, is standing at the counter. He is showing an old German World War II helmet to a customer with neo-Nazi affinities.*

Svetozar (*in a thick accent*)   Yes. This is 250 euros. I can give you for 230. I can not give you for less. Very good value.

Customer   Only, I saw you can get it online for 150.

Svetozar (*in a thick accent*)   150? Impossible. Only fake cost 150. Real thing – 250. Because I like you English, 225. My last . . . (*Louder, in Serbian.*) Željka? How do you say 'offer'?

Željka[2] (*off stage*)   What?

Svetozar[3]   Offer, woman, how do you say it? In English?

Željka   Offer.

Svetozar (*in a thick accent*)   Offer. My last offer. Very, very good price. This is antique. 1942. Very good condition.

Customer   OK. I'll have to think about it and come back.

Svetozar (*in a thick accent*)   OK. You think. But you can not get better. You trust me.

Customer   OK. Thanks for your help.

Customer *leaves.*

Svetozar (*under his breath*)   Go screw yourself, you colonial bastard. He has no money, sure. They looted half the planet, and now he has no money for one helmet.

Željka *enters.*

Željka   What was that?

---

[2] Zeljka speaks Croatian.
[3] Svetozar speaks Serbian except when it says 'in a thick accent' which is when he speaks English.

Svetozar   He's looking at it, examining it, like a monkey with a walnut, and then, get this, he has to think about it.

Željka   Which helmet? The SS one?

Svetozar   Yeah. Not even the most expensive one. He could have had it for 200 Euros.

Željka   That's a lot of money these days. And a helmet isn't even worth it. What's he going to do with a helmet? Wear it around the house? He's shaved his head so people can see who he is, now he's going to hide it under a helmet.

Svetozar   Hang on, he was screwing me around for half an hour! He gets dressed head to toe in the uniform, then he wants some boots, are these size nine, or nine-and-a-half or ten, totally clueless about European sizes, I bend over backwards to be nice to the guy and then he decides he doesn't want them. What am I . . . does it say on my forehead 'Nice guy. Fuck with me'? Are we a charity or something? Huh?

Željka   No, of course we're not. I'm just saying times are hard, everyone's broke and worried about the future. We need to show some solidarity. We're all in the same boat.

Svetozar   Who's in the same boat? Me, in the same boat with these fascists? Never. My granddad didn't survive the Bileća camp so I can be all pally with fascists. We're not in the same boat, oh no. This is just business.

Željka   We're ordinary people. A small business. And the poor bastards who shop here are just as poor as us. I'm just saying we should show some solidarity with them on an economic level. I mean, we're all screwed. Know what I mean?

Svetozar   Well, I loved showing solidarity when we had our little shop. Željkica, d'you remember? We had it so good then, d'you remember?

Željka *thinks.*

Svetozar   When we met. You were so young, a refugee. A scrawny little thing, but a lady. (*He laughs.*) And I was a tramp. A wide boy. Remember our little room in Goethe Strasse?

Željka   I remember.

Svetozar   Didn't we have it good?

Željka   We did.

Svetozar   Didn't we have it all worked out, what we'd do and how we'd do it . . . A restaurant, then, I don't know, a club for our people . . . then put on shows with stars from back home . . .

Željka   When was that, Tozo? It must've been twenty years ago.

Svetozar   Surely not . . .

Željka   Nearly.

They both get lost in thought.

Svetozar   And when we found this place?

Željka   I remember . . .

Svetozar   D'you remember?

Željka   I remember, I remember. How could I forget?

Svetozar   It was your idea. You said, let's open a shop for our people. So they don't have to smuggle Cedevita, Vegeta and Munchmallows into the country. Huh? Isn't that what you said?

Željka   Life's a little easier when you can make sarma and serve a nice bit of cured ham for New Year. I don't know how many times my dad said it – nothing cures a hangover better than a nice jug of cold Cedevita. And God knows our people drink as much here as they do at home.

Svetozar   Even more.

Željka   Even more. You're right. Our people are the first to get shafted. Abroad.

Svetozar   And back home too.

They fall silent.

Željka   You know what? We should stop whining. My sister works double shifts in a supermarket in Zagreb and is allowed only two visits to the toilet and all for a minimum wage. Did you know that at that time of the month they put a plastic bracelet on her so she can go to the toilet more often. What kind of a life is that? In her own country! As for your relatives in Serbia, dogs live better over here than they do over there. What more do we need? Flags are selling like hot cakes. Yesterday I sold two boxes of Christmas baubles with swastikas, those expensive retro ones, and Christmas is more than two months away.

Svetozar   OK, you're right, but still . . .

Željka   Still, shmill. Just keep quiet and hope the government doesn't ban the rally next week. Then we'll have something to complain about.

Svetozar   Huh. You can't say what you think anywhere any more. There's no freedom any more.

Željka   You're right there.

Svetozar   Those days are gone. When I think about how things used to be . . . Before the war.

Željka   Yup. And how we were always complaining about something. Who would have thought what was around the corner.

Svetozar   Yeah. Fools. What a country it was! People used to live so well.

They fall silent. **Željka** *thinks about it. Then she says:*

Željka   Well, some lived better than the others.

Svetozar   Who?

Željka   You know who. Come on, you don't need me to spell it out.

Svetozar   Ah Željka, not that story again, you're as boring as hell.

Željka   Yes, I'm boring. Of course.

Svetozar   Well, when you go on, you just go on and on and on.

Željka   Fine, I go on about it, but the truth is the truth.

Svetozar   What truth, woman?

Željka   You know full well what truth.

Svetozar   Željka . . .

Željka   All the money went to Belgrade, that truth. What truth d'you think?

Svetozar   The money went to Belgrade first and was then equally divided.

Željka   Yeah, most equally to you, and then to Kosovo, and then the rest, the scraps, came back to us. Our own money. I mean really . . .

Svetozar   Oh will you ever stop banging on about it? I've explained it to you a million times, but you don't have the head for economics. That's how the system worked – someone had to be in charge.

Željka   Yeah. And it just had to be you.

Svetozar   Better us than you. As soon as you got the chance you tore the country to pieces.

Željka   We tore the country to pieces?!

Svetozar   And just who was it who was so desperate to secede? Was it me perhaps?

Željka   You suck our blood a hundred years, we couldn't take it any longer.

Svetozar   Željka, I'm warning you, watch it, I know where this is going. . .

Željka   From the beginning, from the very beginning, we were the idealists and you were just sponging off us.

Svetozar   Yeah right, you were the idealists. God save me from your ideals –

Željka   Are you trying to say it wasn't like that? Are you trying to say you didn't have an agenda from the beginning? Why, didn't your granddad –

Svetozar   Leave my granddad out of it, he was a hero –

Željka   Sure he was. Got his medals from a place like this . . .

Svetozar   Željka, leave my granddad alone, you'll get a kicking, I swear –

Željka   OK. Fine.

Silence. They stew. **Željka** *is not sure whether to carry on.*

Željka   True. Alright. It can't be denied. Granddad was a hero.

Svetozar   Yes, he was.

Silence.

Svetozar   Željkica . . .

Željka *remains silent.*

Svetozar   Željkica.

Željka   What?

Svetozar   I'm sorry. I'm sorry, please. I'd never hurt you, you know that.

Željka   I know.

Svetozar   Sure?

Željka   I'm sure.

Svetozar   I swear.

Željka   I know!

Svetozar   Promise me something.

Željka   What?

Svetozar   Promise me that when this all blows over, the crisis and all that, promise me we'll open our Dolly Bell again.

Željka   Oh, Tozo, when will that be?

Svetozar   It'll happen, it bloody will. This can't go on forever.

Željka   Unless something worse happens.

Svetozar   Sometimes you can be really cruel.

Željka   Fine, fine, dear. We'll open Dolly Bell again. Better times will come.

Svetozar   Here he is, the English guy's coming back.

Željka   You see. And you slag him off.

Svetozar   Oh, you know me. Speak before I think –

Željka (*gently*)   Yes, I know you. I'm going to go pack the braces. And you be nice, don't let the cunt have it for less than 200 under any circumstances. Clear?

Svetozar   Clear. Željkica . . .

Željka   Yes?

Svetozar   Do you love me?

Željka *smiles.*

Scene Twenty

German   So I finished my studies, got married and moved
to Dresden. We had a son and in August 1968 we treated
ourselves to a weekend in a bed and breakfast in Karlsbad.
There were West Germans there too. They were friendly at
breakfast – until they realised we were from the East. Then
suddenly there wasn't room at their table any more. We were
about to go out for a walk when we heard the sound of tank
treads. The landlady came in and said through her tears:
you lot are back – your soldiers are back on our streets. It
took me a moment to realise that they were putting down
the Prague Spring. We went out and watched the tanks roll
past, soldiers lining the pavement to ensure a clear passage
for the troops. Our son asked what was going on and a
Russian soldier told him that their little brother in Prague
was unwell and needed help. We packed our bags and while
we were paying for the room the porter whispered to us that
no one was watching the Czech border because everything
was so chaotic – we could cross now if we wanted – tomorrow
it might all be different, we should hurry. We didn't go – I
don't know why. Maybe because on that particular day,
Europe for me was that smug, overweight West German lady
at breakfast who wouldn't let us sit at her table.

Scene Twenty-One

German   Zeus the almighty, king of the gods, slave to his
desires and capable of changing shape if such cunning is
required: to ensnare a woman, has Europa on his back, to
satisfy his lust, somewhere in the West: Crete.

Europa   Zeus the almighty, king of the gods, slave to his
desires and capable of changing shape if such cunning is
required: to ensnare a woman, has Europa on his back, to
satisfy his lust, somewhere in the West: Crete.

Scene Twenty-Two

Woman   So the results came – and all my hopes were dashed.

Yes – they did find one small mutation CHEK2 1100deIC, which means a higher probability of breast cancer, but the mutation itself is so small that they are not going to do anything about it. But I am to look and observe – as if there was anything to look at.

So I look, through a magnifying glass, what else am I to do, but I thought: if I am not an Ashkenazi Jew, then perhaps I can know something more about my genes, if this is so easy. I read in a newspaper that Americans have this huge genetic laboratory. You pay them, then spit into a test-tube, and send it to them, and they can tell you all they know based on the saliva which you spit.

OK. So I spit. Again, waited four weeks, but what the hell, you live once, why should I be restraining myself? If I am not a Jew, maybe there are other mysteries of my Slavic genotype out there.

English Actor   Your maternal Haplogroup: J2b1.

Woman   Correct, it is me – J2b1.

Various Actors   Haplogroup J comprising about 10–20 per cent of the populations of Iraq, Iran, Syria and Palestine, and 25 per cent of the population of the Arabian peninsula. But the haplogroup's history extends far beyond its region of origin – after the development of agriculture 10,000 years ago farmers carried offshoots of the J haplogroup from the Near East to the western fringes of Europe.

Researchers who recently disinterred the body of the fourteenth-century Italian poet Petrarch tested his mitochondrial DNA and found that it belonged to J2, a major branch of haplogroup J.

Today, J2a can be found among about 4 per cent of people living in Denmark and northern Germany. It is also found in England and parts of Scotland,

Woman   First thing I did to understand all this, I logged on the forum of my haplogroup – J2b1. I wrote, 'Hey there, I am J2b1. Are there any other J2b1s here?' These are the answers I got . . .

Various Actors   I am J2b1 and my maternal line goes back to (northeastern) Spain at the turn of the nineteenth to twentieth centuries.

I am J2b1, my maternal line is Russian (centre of Russia: Niznhy Novgorod/Vyatka (Kirov) area. Last names: Pyankov, Blinov, Satayev.

I am also J2b1. My oldest ancestress Margaret Lynch was from Cork, Ireland and in Newport R.I. by 1860.

Hello, Iam J2b1, I'm French and my maternal line goes back to west of France since the seventeenth century.

I am also J2b1 . . . My parents are from south of Turkey. I lived in Istanbul and living both in Berlin and Istanbul now.

I am also J2b1. My earliest known ancestry goes back to England on the maternal side. Names arc Holmes, Hart, Marriott, White and goes back to 1719 near Wilden in Woods, Bedfordshire, England.

I am fascinated by all your responses because most of you have European ancestry. I am also J2b1, but I am from Republic of Georgia, Mountain Jew (Google it) and my recent ancestors are from Georgia/Azerbaijan. Mountain Jews in the former Soviet Union supposedly came from Iran (via mountains), hence the name.

I am J2b1. My grandmother also used to tell me about her grandmother who was the daughter of a powerful man who went by the name of Omer Pasha (or Omer Aga), who was from the Balkans.

There don't seem to be many of us J2b1b! Here are some of
my mother's ancestors – as J2b1b comes from Germany etc,
I have gathered the names of the families in Germany in the
nineteenth century: Gobel, Zurfass, Kuhn, Stilz, Schweitzer,
Botsch.

J2b1. I intuited that my distant relatives migrated from
Mesopotamia through Yemen to Azerbaijan, then via raft to
Finland, down to the Celtic British Isles, finally emigrating
to the United States.

Scene Twenty-Three

Ana's *body with protruding stomach is positioned on the stretcher
across an aeroplane seat. Around her are passengers on a scheduled
flight.*

They are sitting, reading newspapers.

Official   While they were immobilising her with self-
adhesive tape, Ana did not manage to close her eyes. One
eyelid remained open, stuck to her eyebrow. It remained
open and stuck for the following twenty-six hours it took to
transport Ana to an undisclosed location.

Aircraft Official   Ladies and gentlemen, we are currently
flying through an area of turbulence. For your own safety
please remain in your seats and fasten your seatbelts. We
apologise for any inconvenience.

Official   A careful examination of the documents in Mishal
Khan's file which has been maintained by the British Secret
Service since 2003 led to the conclusion that Mishal Khan
had been in contact with terrorist groups active in Great
Britain and Pakistan on at least three separate occasions. On
six separate occasions Mishal Khan stayed with his relative
Fatima Al Usrah in the German city of Ulm, one of the
centres of Islamic radicalism in Germany. Fatima Al Usrah,
born in Pakistan, has been on the list of closely observed
German Muslims for years because of the large number of

visits she receives from people, mainly male, from Pakistan and Jordan.

Foreign Official   Combined British and Croatian intelligence suggests that Mishal Khan had on at least one occasion, on his trip to Bosnia, visited homes related to a member of a radical muslim group, the Bosnian *Vehabije*. Mrs Khans's knowledge of and involvment in the matter to date remains unclear.

Passenger 1   Do you mean this, erm . . . wrapped-up person? Well yes, I noticed, how could I not notice. We were on this flight by accident. I mean our flight was cancelled and then it was a question of whether we should stay another day in London, or whether we should, erm . . . transfer. So I say to Slavica, come on let's stay, seeing as this has happened, I mean, I say, let's stay, why not . . . they'll put us up in a hotel. Yes, but they were going to put us in a hotel at the airport. It's not like back home in Zagreb where you get to the centre in twenty minutes. Here you have to drive for an hour and a half and, also, Slavica, she hates packing and unpacking. She could hardly shut her suitcase, she'd bought so much stuff, bless her. And then we told them to put us on the alternative flight. So we shouldn't even have been on that flight, if you know what I mean. So I really don't know what to say. I mean, it's not OK to Sellotape a pregnant woman so she can't move, no it's not. But then, who knows who she is and what she's done. She must've done something. But to do it like that, well, I don't know what to tell you. It's a bit out of order. That's all.

Passenger 2 (*in German*)   I don't understand. Was it a deportation?

Passenger 3   I think it's intolerable.

After all, I pay my taxes. At the end of the day we all know that the budget of European countries for national security is enormous. If that person is really responsible for something, or suspected of some terrorist act, then she should be transported in an appropriate manner. Not in a way which brings us all into a situation where we become participants in something about which we have no idea and nobody is telling us anything. Surely there's a proper procedure?

Passenger 4   I think it was performance art.

Passenger 5   No comment.

Passenger 6   Well . . . I have nothing to say, but I agree with my husband.

Passenger 7   You know, it was terrible. I'll never forget it. I mean all those people pretending that nothing was happening. Awful. I mean, in whose name are they doing this? They say it's happening throughout Europe. Has anyone put this in their election manifesto, the abolishment of human rights? No, no, terrible, we should have done something.

Stewardess   They just told us she was travelling with us to Frankfurt and we shouldn't speak to her. Yes, it was rather uncomfortable. And the passengers were wondering, and some were asking me, I mean, my God, as if I'm some kind of . . . world president . . . I mean, my bosses only told me, what could I do . . .

Journalist 1   Judges at Europe's top human rights court will on Wednesday October fifth hear the first case to come before them arising from the US CIA's program of extraordinary rendition, the campaign of covert cross-border transfers of terror suspects, supported by a network of cross European intelligence agencies. The case has been brought by Mr and Mrs Khan, a British and Croatian citizen who were abducted by what they claim to be British agents in London in 2010, and transferred to CIA custody in a Kabul dungeon.

During the two and four months respectively they spent in captivity neither of the two were brought before a judge or charged.

Journalist 2   Mrs Khan was released a few days before her due date and flown back to Great Britain where she gave birth to a healthy baby girl on May first 2010.

Mr Khan was subsequently released having been found innocent of all allegations made against him. A compelling body of evidence corroborating Mr and Mrs Khan's story suggests that their haunting captivity was a result of no more than a case of mistaken identity.

Journalist 3   Following allegations of terrorist affiliation, both Mr and Mrs Khan have been dismissed from their positions at the Institute of Marine Biochemistry. We have discovered that the responsible agencies were suspicious of Mr and Mrs Khan from the very start of their acquaintance and that the police intervened on the night of twenty-first June 2005 in the German city of Dresden where Ana, née Omerpašić and Mishal Khan attempted to burn down the hotel in which they were staying. Whether the convention of young European chemists they were both attending was just a cover for terrorist activities, remains unclear.

Scene Twenty-Four

J2b1   Well . . . I am Greek. In case you're interested here are the results of my gene test from iGenea . . . damn this cost me $215 . . . J2b1 found in Italy, Greece, Anatolia Turkey, some Semites, and Balkans and is rumored to have ancient origin. My natural hair colour is more brownish sorta . . . I also have blue eyes. Here is a picture of me . . .

You look like you could come from any place in Europe. I would've guessed Central Europe. I don't think you look like the quintessential Greek though.

I am J2b1. My father's father's mother came from the Zidan family, which was an Arab tribe from the Galilee in Palestine. They were prominent in Tiberias, by the Sea of Galilee, and one of the patriarchs was Daher Umar Zidan, who led local insurgencies against Ottoman rule. There is a mosque in Tiberias called the Zidani mosque.

Hello, I am J2b1a2 and I am Dutch and all my female ancestors, known until 1600 were Dutch.

Woman   Who am I then? A French-German-Dutch-Irish-British-Turkish-Italian-Russian-Hungarian-Scottish-Georgian-Jewish-Spanish woman with small boobs.

Scene Twenty-Five

Shaman   Donald Tusk – the Polish Prime Minister – picks a card with a bear. The very first thing that comes to his mind is that a bear is better than a frog, but only then he can hear a voice of a ghost: 'Enter the cage, Prime Minister Tusk, where silence surrounds my wisdom – the bear says. It is time to take a look into one's own interior, time to digest all the experience and set new goals.'

Have I ever stopped listening to myself? – Prime Minister wonders. Have I been asking others for the answers to the questions that tormented me? Have I lost the power of cognition? Why do I feel so confused? Where did my clear thoughts go? Where did the honey of life go, the one I miss so much?

Prime Minister of Poland understands it is time to enter the cabin of dreams. He knows it is time to close one's eyes and say goodbye to the illusion. The cabin of dreams closes.

Prime Ministers steps on the path of silence. He calms his thoughts. Now he is listening to the answers. Journalists of all the big newspapers, the left-wing ones, and the right-wing ones, go out of their offices and enter the cabin of dreams. The directors of big banks and corporations, priests, bishops, and the primate follow him. There is a cabin of dreams waiting for everyone. This is the night when life in Poland stops. Everyone who can do it, takes the arm of the bear, they cuddle up to its fluffy fur and fall asleep to wake up with the answer.

Scene Twenty-Six

German   Europe, a long-lost love, who'd twice tucked a note with her address on it into my pocket that I hadn't found, couldn't read, or simply didn't have the confidence to turn up at hers. How would she have received me? Who would have opened the door to me?

Others did go. In trains that didn't stop as they trundled through Dresden station, accompanied by the cheers or jeers of those who weren't allowed to go to Europe. I wasn't there. I wasn't on Bernauer Street when the Wall came down on the ninth of November. I was in Berlin, in the Schönhauserstrasse, in my son's flat, in bed with flu – whilst he, surrounded by crowds, edged his way across the border. I lay awake and heard the city buzzing. I could have got myself up and joined in but I didn't. I had courted this woman all my life, chastely, awkwardly. I didn't want to meet her in amongst a bellowing crowd of my fellow Germans. I didn't want to meet her in a pub, but on a summer's night by the sea, in a small harbour town where a band would be playing in the marketplace and people, dressed in their best, were dancing under fairy lights.

Scene Twenty-Seven

Singers   'Soave sia il vento, tranquille sia l'onda'
  'Ed ognie le mento
  Be-ni-gno ri-sponda'

Christopher   My mother used to sing it with my father.

Astrid   *Pst!*

Singers   'ai no – stride-sir.
   Soave sia il vento, tranquille la sia l'onda.'

Christopher   I've sung both the bass and the soprano line.
The room was packed, everyone stood – we were
accompanied on a piano.

Astrid   Be quiet. That was really quite magnificent. The
interface between music and image was sublime.

Christopher *and* **Sunčana** *alone.*

Christopher   It's a bit kitschy I suppose in this form.

Sunčana   It makes me feel sick.

Christopher   Ah, but isn't beauty like that? Doesn't it sort of
upset us, reproach us? Because it makes us think life could
be better and then when it stops . . .

Sunčana   Harmony cannot occur without justice.

Christopher   Then we'd better stop making music! Yeah,
brings it all back, my first visit to Europe, with my school, on
tour, acting, all of us in this minibus, we were young, I was
young once. Performing *Hamlet* in Elsinore, *Romeo and Juliet*
in Verona, *The Merchant of Venice*. In Venice. Completely fell
for this . . . continent, gave my life to it, even if it doesn't
always . . . well – deliver the goods.

Sunčana   You know what they should show, in their film?
They should show a Somali kid beaten blind by the Golden
Dawn. They should show a banker pissing in the eyes of a
homeless guy in London.

Christopher   No. No, that's crude, reductive.

Sunčana   They should show Moroccans sleeping in
polytunnels in Spain. Show Marine Le Pen's smile and Geert
Wilders smile and Anders Breivik –

Christopher   Now, now you're wilfully confusing the worst with the best –

Sunčana   They should show the Danube thick with chemicals, or an *indignado* in Madrid, or maybe a teenage girl from Moldova trafficked into, where, Ipswich – yes, show all these things with that music, then that would be something to see – what do you think, Christopher?

Christopher   I tell you what I think, I think the task's harder actually, I think we have to make the case for Europe being something magnificent and OK, maybe we've reduced it to bribes and bungs and trade barriers –

Sunčana   The sniffer dogs, the dying towns, the dead currencies, the bodies in the sea.

Christopher   Oh, and the architecture, and, OK, the prosperity – yes: fifty uninterrupted years – and the lifting up of the Southern nations, and the re-built devastated cities –

Sunčana   Yes, yes, the fucking Commissionaires on their high-speed trains – the Credit Agencies flying in to write off whole nations –

Christopher   Don't we always expect too much? We always want perfection and OK, we get muddle and it is a muddle –

Sunčana   – yeah show you, and your colleagues, the political class moving from one espresso to another at your funerals in Shropshire and your sentimental shit about something that never existed.

Christopher   Look, who are you exactly?

Astrid   What – what's going on?

Christopher   Our friend here has been deceiving us.

Astrid   Sunčana?

Christopher   Is that even your name? What are you?

Sunčana   OK. Call me an artist. Say I make films, or I make events, or maybe I create . . . happenings. Say this is one right now.

Christopher   I see. And what would be the subject of this . . . happening?

Sunčana   Oh, all the big ideas. Fear. And lies. And false hope, definitely that. In fact, why not sing for us? You love Europe so much, you love culture so much, now's your chance. Sing for us.

Astrid   I'll get security.

Christopher   Don't . . . bother.

Astrid   I think you brought her in.

Christopher   Yes. That's right. All my fault, probably.

Sunčana   They'll sack you now.

Christopher   Very likely.

Sunčana   Why don't you sing then?

Christopher   Why not? Nothing to lose, nothing to be ashamed of.

Sunčana   Nothing to lose, Christopher?

Christopher, *unaccompanied, sings the bass part of 'Soave sia il vento'. He stops.*

Christopher   Happy now?

Scene Twenty-Eight

Officer   Right, according to Regulation 2003/343/CE, Lebanese asylum applicants can stay in the first country of entry – that means Greece. No go Germany, no go England, no go Poland. Got it?

Well, Europa, I can't promise anything. We'll just have to see what we can do, OK? But you can stay for now.

Europa   Crete, where he transforms himself into an eagle in order to conceive children with Europa, children who will rule Crete, where her son's son will have a bull's head: the Minotaur – not divine – misshapen, confined to a labyrinth built for him by the best of the best – the grandson of Europa, roaring in the darkness, tearing human flesh in the vaults of the tremendous palace – the return of the divine as nightmare, which began so radiantly with Europa, the lady from the land of plenty.

Scene Twenty-Nine

English 1   An Englishman goes into a German pub and says to the Pole serving behind the bar. . .

German 1   I believe I forgot to mention that this joke shouldn't have any stereotypes in it.

English 1   You're not serious?

German 1   No stereotypes.

English 1   Would you mind if I just finish telling the joke first?

German 2   No, it won't do. It implies that the English are a nation of drunks.

Polish 1   They are.

English 2   I'm allowed to say that. I'm English.

German 1   But Germans drink too.

English 2   That's why I said it was a German pub.

Croatian 1   Anyway, the beer tastes better in Germany.

Polish 1   What's with the Pole behind the bar? Because we only do the crap jobs?

German 1   Because you're not as rude as German bar staff.

English 1   All right then. A German comes into an English pub and says to the Pole behind the bar . . .

German 2   Germans don't like English beer.

English 2   That's prejudice.

German 2   No, it is just an expirience.

Polish 2   So wherever you go, it's still a Polish woman serving you. How come?

English 2   Realism. Have you any idea how many Poles work in the UK? Anyway I never said the Pole was a woman, that's sexist – it could be a man.

Polish 2   Unlikely.

Croatian 2   I think the joke should at least have one Croatian in it.

German 1   A Pole goes into a Yugoslavian restaurant.

Croatian 1   No such thing any more.

German 2   Well, I've never heard of a Croatian restaurant. Do you have those in Poland?

Polish 1   No, definitely not. We don't even have Croatians.

English 1   What have you got in Croatia that we could put in a joke?

Croatian 1   Our government.

Croatian 1   That was a joke.

Polish 1   I think the joke should take place in Poland.

English 1   A Croatian goes into an English restaurant in Poland.

German 1   English food? Is there such a thing as English cuisine?

English 2   Curry.

German 2   We can't talk about India in a European play.

English 1   But India is the future.

DRAMA ONLINE

A new way to study drama

From curriculum classics
to contemporary writing
Accompanied by
theory and practice

Discover. Read.
Study. Perform.

Find out more:
www.dramaonlinelibrary.com

 FOLLOW US ON TWITTER @DRAMAONLINELIB

Bloomsbury Methuen Drama Modern Plays

include work by

Bola Agbaje
Edward Albee
Davey Anderson
Jean Anouilh
John Arden
Peter Barnes
Sebastian Barry
Alistair Beaton
Brendan Behan
Edward Bond
William Boyd
Bertolt Brecht
Howard Brenton
Amelia Bullmore
Anthony Burgess
Leo Butler
Jim Cartwright
Lolita Chakrabarti
Caryl Churchill
Lucinda Coxon
Curious Directive
Nick Darke
Shelagh Delaney
Ishy Din
Claire Dowie
David Edgar
David Eldridge
Dario Fo
Michael Frayn
John Godber
Paul Godfrey
James Graham
David Greig
John Guare
Mark Haddon
Peter Handke
David Harrower
Jonathan Harvey
Iain Heggie

Robert Holman
Caroline Horton
Terry Johnson
Sarah Kane
Barrie Keeffe
Doug Lucie
Anders Lustgarten
David Mamet
Patrick Marber
Martin McDonagh
Arthur Miller
D. C. Moore
Tom Murphy
Phyllis Nagy
Anthony Neilson
Peter Nichols
Joe Orton
Joe Penhall
Luigi Pirandello
Stephen Poliakoff
Lucy Prebble
Peter Quilter
Mark Ravenhill
Philip Ridley
Willy Russell
Jean-Paul Sartre
Sam Shepard
Martin Sherman
Wole Soyinka
Simon Stephens
Peter Straughan
Kate Tempest
Theatre Workshop
Judy Upton
Timberlake Wertenbaker
Roy Williams
Snoo Wilson
Frances Ya-Chu Cowhig
Benjamin Zephaniah

Bloomsbury Methuen Drama Contemporary Dramatists

include

John Arden (two volumes)
Arden & D'Arcy
Peter Barnes (three volumes)
Sebastian Barry
Mike Bartlett
Dermot Bolger
Edward Bond (eight volumes)
Howard Brenton (two volumes)
Leo Butler
Richard Cameron
Jim Cartwright
Caryl Churchill (two volumes)
Complicite
Sarah Daniels (two volumes)
Nick Darke
David Edgar (three volumes)
David Eldridge (two volumes)
Ben Elton
Per Olov Enquist
Dario Fo (two volumes)
Michael Frayn (four volumes)
John Godber (four volumes)
Paul Godfrey
James Graham
David Greig
John Guare
Lee Hall (two volumes)
Katori Hall
Peter Handke
Jonathan Harvey (two volumes)
Iain Heggie
Israel Horovitz
Declan Hughes
Terry Johnson (three volumes)
Sarah Kane
Barrie Keeffe
Bernard-Marie Koltès (two volumes)
Franz Xaver Kroetz
Kwame Kwei-Armah
David Lan
Bryony Lavery
Deborah Levy
Doug Lucie

David Mamet (four volumes)
Patrick Marber
Martin McDonagh
Duncan McLean
David Mercer (two volumes)
Anthony Minghella (two volumes)
Tom Murphy (six volumes)
Phyllis Nagy
Anthony Neilson (two volumes)
Peter Nichol (two volumes)
Philip Osment
Gary Owen
Louise Page
Stewart Parker (two volumes)
Joe Penhall (two volumes)
Stephen Poliakoff (three volumes)
David Rabe (two volumes)
Mark Ravenhill (three volumes)
Christina Reid
Philip Ridley (two volumes)
Willy Russell
Eric-Emmanuel Schmitt
Ntozake Shange
Sam Shepard (two volumes)
Martin Sherman (two volumes)
Christopher Shinn
Joshua Sobel
Wole Soyinka (two volumes)
Simon Stephens (three volumes)
Shelagh Stephenson
David Storey (three volumes)
C. P. Taylor
Sue Townsend
Judy Upton
Michel Vinaver (two volumes)
Arnold Wesker (two volumes)
Peter Whelan
Michael Wilcox
Roy Williams (four volumes)
David Williamson
Snoo Wilson (two volumes)
David Wood (two volumes)
Victoria Wood

For a complete catalogue
of Bloomsbury Methuen Drama
titles write to:

Bloomsbury Methuen Drama
Bloomsbury Publishing Plc
50 Bedford Square
London WC1B 3DP

or you can visit our website at:
www.bloomsbury.com/drama